Adventures in Grammarland

Paul Georgiou & Christopher Prendergast

Published by Panarc International Ltd in 2014

Copyright Paul Georgiou and Christopher Prendergast

Illustrations by Daria Mitchell

First Edition

*The authors assert the moral right
under the Copyright, Designs and Patents Act 1988
to be identified at the authors of this work.*

*All Rights reserved.
No part of this publication may be reproduced,
stored in a retrieval system or transmitted, in any form or by any means
without the prior written consent of the authors,
nor be otherwise circulated in any form of binding or cover
other than that which is published
and without a similar condition being imposed on the subsequent purchaser.*

www.panarcpublishing.com

*Panarc International Ltd
(www.panarc.com)*

*ISBN: 978-0-9548740-4-9
Ebook: 978-0-9548740-5-6*

Contents

1. IN THE BEGINNING 1
2. THE DOOR 4
3. GRAMMARLAND 6
4. "WORDS USE PEOPLE" 9
5. AN ARGUMENT 13
6. THE ODDEST OF MEETINGS 18
7. SOME FURRY FRIENDS 23
8. SYNTAX TAKES CONTROL 26
9. "THE GREAT CONFLAGRATION" 28
10. MORE ABOUT GRAMMARLAND 37
11. PREPARATIONS 40
12. THE QUEST BEGINS 43
13. THE BOG OF DISUSE 49
14. CAMPFIRES 52
15. THE GIANT OATH 59
16. MISUSE 66
17. TAUTOLOGY AND FAMILY 72
18. THE RIVER OF TIME 83
19. FORTRESS DUR 91
20. THE SUBTERRANEAN CAVES 95
21. EVIL OBSERVED 104
22. A LESSON LEARNED 106
23. ION, THE RIDDLEMAN 109
24. THE BATTLE BEGINS 117
25. THE TAKING OF MELISA 125
26. MELISA'S PASSING 131
27. THE MIGHTY SHREDDER 132
28. THE FINAL CONFRONTATION 138
29. THE VICTORS REJOICE 146
30. THE END 149

1. In the Beginning

"It is the end." It was an old man's voice, quaking with fear and foreboding, but tinged with anger. The sound seemed to come from far away, and yet those four words rang out clear as a bell. "It is the end." Then, there was a crash like a thousand distant thunderclaps all meeting in one place, followed by the rumbling of a great building disintegrating beneath the onslaught of irresistible forces. The noise gradually subsided, as dust settles after a vast explosion, until, for a moment, there was silence. "Save us", "Help us", "We must not all die", a dozen cries of lingering hope broke the stillness. But then came the wind and the rain, mere gusts at first but soon turning into a howling storm, blowing away the forlorn cries of those troubled souls, just as the waking mind coldly unravels and dispels a dream.

Very slowly Josh removed the flute from his lips and looked cautiously around the room. All seemed normal. He was in the library. The sun was shining through the windows. He could hear birds singing in the garden outside. And his father was sitting behind the old mahogany desk.

"You're definitely improving," said Mr Ware, putting down the book he had been reading.

"What!", said Josh.

"The flute," Mr Ware explained. "You will soon have mastered those scales."

"Oh! right," Josh agreed.

Obviously, and yet unbelievably, his father had heard nothing - except Josh's flute exercises.

"Anyway, you'd better put it away now. Your mother and I are going to the meeting at your school. Mrs Brown will be here as usual to keep an eye on things. We probably won't be back until quite late, so make sure you're in bed and asleep when we come in."

Josh placed his flute in its old black case. Carefully he returned the case to its accustomed space on the shelf, at the end of the small section of the library that his father had given him for his own books. The flute with its odd wooden mouthpiece had belonged to Josh's father, and his father before him, and Mr Ware had said that one day, perhaps, Josh would pass it on to a son of his own.

Josh, still perplexed by his extraordinary experience, shook his head. The noise had been deafening and the cries for help desperate. He must have imagined it. And yet he had never heard strange voices before. And they had seemed so real, as though their owners had known he might be there and were calling out to him.

Josh's father, who was now standing in the doorway of the library, called to his wife: "They hold these parent-teacher meetings at the most inconvenient times." Mrs Ware stopped chatting to Mrs Brown and replied; "This one really is very important. I even postponed a meeting with my publisher so that we could both go. Surely you don't mind giving up a few hours?"

"No, of course I don't mind, Barbara," Mr Ware answered a little grumpily. He was straightening his tie in the mirror that hung just inside the library door. On the floor, beneath the mirror, in its usual resting place, stood the ancient walking stick, capped with the finely-chiselled silver head of an old man. The stick, like the flute, had been in Mr Ware's family for many generations and, although it had not enjoyed much exercise recently, it had accompanied Mr Ware's father on many a long country walk until his death three years before. "I don't mind in the least. It's just that I have so much to do."

"The busiest people always have the most time," Mrs Ware teased.

"That was said by a very clever, lazy person simply to encourage someone less clever but more industrious to work even harder."

"'Sounds like a fair description to me," Mrs Ware replied. Whereupon, both Josh's parents burst into laughter.

2. The Door

After tea, Mrs Brown settled down in front of the television. Josh liked Mrs Brown but it had always seemed to him that the only thing she kept her eye on when she stayed for an evening was 'the box'. Or was it the other way round? Perhaps it was the television, with its great single eye and a thousand voices, which kept watch over Mrs Brown. ("There's nothing wrong with the boy's imagination," Josh could hear his form-master telling his parents. "Nothing wrong in that department. Oh, my word, no!")

At nine o'clock, in a break between programmes, Mrs Brown said to Josh: "Isn't it time you were off to bed?" "I suppose so," Josh conceded and complied. He would spend half an hour playing with his games console in his room and then go to sleep.

About half past ten, Josh awoke feeling thirsty. He slipped out of bed, put on his dressing-gown and crept quietly downstairs. He could hear the muffled voices from the television as he passed the door of the living room. When he reached the kitchen, he opened the refrigerator, poured himself an extremely large glass of orange squash and drank it in a series of long gulps. He felt much better.

It was as he returned along the passageway, as he passed

the library door, that he heard, for the second time that day, a strange voice. At first he thought it must be coming from the television in the living room. But the living room was on the left side of the passage - and the voice came from the right. Josh stopped and listened.

"Oh dear!" said the voice, "Why do they waste so much time arguing with each other? This continual bickering is entirely senseless."

With the greatest care and even greater caution, Josh turned the handle of the library door and gently opened it.

3. *Grammarland*

"Well, are you coming or going?" said the voice. Josh could see very little in the gloom of the library but, as his eyes became accustomed to the half light, he was able to make out a shape in the corner beside the door. "Please shut the door," said the same voice, "and do stop dithering. There really is no reason to be afraid."

Reason or not, Josh was afraid. The voice seemed to be coming from the silver-capped walking stick - and walking sticks can't talk. But Josh was also curious. And his curiosity conquered his fear. Josh stepped into the library and closed the door.

"That's better," said the walking stick (for it was indeed the walking stick, or rather the silver head at the top of the stick which was speaking). "It's difficult enough to get away from all the arguing in here without having to listen to the television in the living room."

"What... Who are you?" said a still nervous Josh, who, despite the gloom, could now see clearly the silver face on the walking stick.

"What do you mean," snapped the face, "what, who am I? In the first place, which is, after all, an excellent place to begin, you really ought to take a grip on your Interrogative Pronouns. Do you mean 'what' or do you mean 'who' - or do you mean both?"

"I'm terribly sorry," said Josh pertly, surprising himself with his own audacity, "but I had always thought you were a walking stick - not a talking stick."

"I see," the voice returned, "a boy with a taste for quips and rhymes. Rather like.....never mind. I abhor insolence, although I concede it can be a sign of spirit and of that we shall surely have need. Nevertheless, there is no excuse for sloppy thinking. A walking stick indeed! If I may descend to the level of your own juvenile humour, you have, I suggest, taken hold of the wrong end of the stick. How, young man, would you feel if I described you as 'flesh and bone' or, perhaps more perspicaciously, 'stuff and nonsense'! I may look like a walking stick. Indeed I may even be a walking stick. But I am not merely a walking stick - any more than you are just stuff and nonsense."

"I'm sorry," said Josh. "I did not intend to be rude."

"Very well," said the voice. "I will forgive you on this occasion, 'though I think you should know that leniency in such matters is not a quality with which I am usually associated. Permit me to introduce myself. My name is Syntax."

Josh thought Syntax was a very strange name - but he did not say what he thought for he suspected that such a remark would provoke yet another rebuke.

"Should I say Mr. Syntax, Sir?" asked Josh, hoping that he sounded suitably deferential.

"You may address me as Mr. Syntax, Sir - or indeed as Sir Syntax, or Professor Syntax, or Dr. Syntax, or Lord Syntax. It is a matter of total indifference to me. Syntax on its own is to be preferred, since that is my name and, although I have many honorary titles, I have no need of them. That said, I need hardly add - no abbreviations."

Josh wondered what he should say next. He suspected that anything he said might give offence.

"Where am I?" he hazarded. "I mean I know I am in the library, but am I awake or am I dreaming?"

"That is not a very logical set of questions," responded Syntax. "Do you mean 'Where am I?' or do you mean 'What state am I in?' Or rather 'What condition am I in?' Note, boy, that I prefer 'condition' to 'state' because 'state' could indicate either 'place' or 'condition'. It is always better to say precisely what you mean, rather than to leave it to the judgement or guesswork of others. Are you with me, boy?"

"Well, I'm certainly with you in one sense, since I seem to be standing beside you, but I'm not sure I understand you, if that's what you mean?"

Syntax looked at Josh quizzically, uncertain whether the boy was being clever or rude - or both.

"You asked where you are," said Syntax stiffly, his uncertainty still unresolved. "I will tell you. You are in the Library, the Gateway to Grammarland and I, Syntax, Defender of the Laws, Master of Words, Governor of the Sentence (all ancient honorary titles, boy), am its Guardian.

4. "Words Use People"

Josh's head was in a whirl. It had been a very odd day. He looked back towards the library door through which he had entered. The door had disappeared. All he could see was row upon row of books. "Where is the door?" he blurted out.

Adventures in Grammarland

"There are many doors," said Syntax rather pompously, "and as one door shuts, my boy, another opens."

"Yes, but where is my door - the door to the Library?" Josh persisted.

"Hmm", returned Syntax and then, as though he felt this response inadequate, he said "Hmm" again.

Josh knew that he must not panic. And he knew he must not shout. Instead, he said very quietly, "It has been a great pleasure to meet you, Mr. Syntax, but now I think I should like to return to my bed."

"Bed!" exclaimed Syntax, "You can talk of bed when there are adventures to be had, villains to be fought, battles to be won, victories to be claimed."

"Well, you see, I promised my parents that I would be in bed when they came back."

"Have no fear, at least on that account," instructed Syntax, "They will fully understand. And, if not, they will forgive. In any case, assuming you return from the Quest, we can put you back in your bed in good time. Indeed, if you like, we can put you back in your bed before you got up to have a drink of orange squash. You see Grammarland is not subject to the same temporal considerations as those which obtain outside. It is merely a matter of changing the odd tense."

Not really knowing where to begin, Josh picked on one word which caused him particular concern. "What do you mean 'assuming' I return?"

"My dear boy", said Syntax, hopping forward on his stem like a pogo-stick, "you cannot have an adventure without danger. And, if things should not go well, you will at least know, if only briefly, that you have given yourself in a great cause."

"But..." was all Josh managed to utter. Before he could continue, Syntax silenced him with "Shh!". "There they go again," he said with a mixture of impatience and despair. "Put these on," instructed Syntax, indicating, with a nod of his head, a pair of silver-framed spectacles which had appeared on the small table beneath the Library mirror, "and come with me. We must see what we can do."

"But I have perfectly good eye-sight," Josh objected.

"You may have perfectly good eyesight on the other side of the

Library door but, as a boy in Grammarland, you will certainly need these."

Josh remained unconvinced.

"In your world," explained Syntax "people use words to communicate with each other. Here it is the other way round."

"What do you mean - 'the other way round'?" asked Josh, completely puzzled, "Words use people? That is nonsense."

"Words use people," repeated Syntax, evidently relieved that Josh had grasped his point. "Precisely. Words use people and, indeed, other living creatures. These glasses have rather special lenses. They will help you to see what I mean and, as I said, they will help you to see what we can do. Trust me."

Reluctantly Josh put on the glasses.

"And you had better take from the Library something that belongs to you. Just one thing," added Syntax.

"But why?" asked Josh.

"If you don't have something with you from your world, it may be rather difficult to return you to it if the Quest succeeds."

Once again, Josh was not entirely happy with Syntax's answer. What did 'rather difficult' mean? And what did 'if' mean?

"What should I take?" Josh enquired, since he thought he had better make a careful choice if so much depended on it.

"Anything that belongs to you. Preferably something that has been in your family for a long time and that is now yours. Something deeply embedded in your life," replied Syntax, and then added casually, "Your flute, perhaps."

Josh took the small flute from its black box and placed it into the pocket of his dressing gown.

"Good," said Syntax. "Now, let us go."

Syntax bounced ahead of Josh towards the centre of the Library. At every step Josh took, the Library grew larger and, although he knew he must be moving towards the centre of the room, it was nevertheless evident that the centre of the room was getting further away. Indeed, the entire space which had been the Library was expanding so quickly that all the familiar objects (the rows of book-filled shelves, his father's desk and chair) were fast receding from Josh's view, mere distant blurs at the edge of an entirely unfamiliar landscape. The familiar dull green carpet of the library floor was taking on a richer hue of green and the very texture of the carpet was changing as thousands of carpet threads broke from the woven pattern and began to sprout in clumps. The shifting space, the changing colours and, most of all, the writhing carpet beneath his feet conspired to make Josh feel slightly sick.

Josh made an effort to overcome his feelings of panic and, peering hard through the spectacles which Syntax had given him, he desperately tried to bring his new surroundings into focus. After a few moments, he realised that he could see clearly enough. It was less a problem of seeing, more a problem of believing what he saw.

They were now moving through grass, still wet with morning dew. Around them were the trees of an English wood, mostly ash, beech, birch and oak. No birds sang and the only sound to break the silence of the morning was the bickering voices of which Syntax had earlier complained.

After some minutes, these same voices grew louder until, as Josh stepped (and his companion hopped) out of the wood into open countryside, they came upon the most extraordinary gathering.

5. An Argument

"If we are to go on the Quest," said **Pride**, "then we Nouns must be the leaders." This blunt bid for power brought cries of protest from the other parts of speech. "Typical," said **Quickly** dismissively, an Adverb never slow to respond to an insult, or anything else for that matter.

"Now listen," said **Pride** ponderously. "My reasoning on this matter is simple - simple enough for even the flightiest of Adverbs to grasp. We Nouns have the closest and most direct link with the world. We represent everything that is. If we are to succeed in the Quest, surely it is obvious that the Nouns have the best qualifications for leadership. After all, the thing we seek, if it exists, will be, must be, one of us - that is, a Noun". **Pride** preened himself at the subtlety of this last proposition. 'Let's see how they deal with that', **Pride** thought.

"I support **Pride**," said **Blind**, an Adjective distinguished more by loyalty than intelligence. "There will be many dangers on the way and I for one would like to know that the strongest Words are at the front."

Josh looked on in amazement. "Who are these, these...?" he

trailed off, because he did not know how to describe the creatures he saw before him.

"Words, dear boy, Words, Words," whispered Syntax. "Nothing but Words."

"It seems to me, **Blind**," snapped **Gruffly**, an Adverb chiefly remarkable for his generally insensitive nature, "that you are not only sightless but brainless. What do you mean the 'strongest' Words? Are you suggesting that Nouns are stronger than Verbs? Have you ever seen a Noun do anything without the help of a Verb? Even the most powerful Nouns are impotent without the Verbs. Everything a Noun achieves, everything he says or does, is accomplished through the good offices of the Verbs."

"He's right," said **To Gloat**, the first Verb to speak since Josh and Syntax had been close enough to hear what was being said. "If you want anything done, I think I can say without fear of contradiction that you Nouns are entirely dependent on us Verbs."

Pride, who had heard this argument a thousand times before, remained undeterred. "A Verb", he stated in a tone that implied he was about to reveal a self-evident truth, "a Verb needs one of two things, or both, before it can do anything. It always needs a 'doer' and, in most cases, a 'done to', that is, a Subject and an Object: in short, it needs Nouns. Furthermore, as you well know, it is the duty of a Verb to agree with a Noun, whenever a Noun assumes the status of a Subject. Since we Nouns represent all reality, since you Verbs are, as I have demonstrated, impotent without us, and since on most occasions you Verbs are duty-bound to agree with us, my case is proved."

The speakers in this strange debate were the oddest creatures Josh had ever seen. **Pride** and **To Gloat**, who were the tallest of the Words, came up to Josh's shoulder. **Blind** stood no higher than Josh's waist. Some of the others, who had yet to speak, were much smaller. And they came in all shapes. **Pride** who wore a purple uniform, with epaulets, medals and buttons of brightly-shining gold, looked like a miniature military man; he stood stiffly and looked about haughtily. **To Gloat**, whose face bore a permanently supercilious, self-satisfied expression, was dressed in a suit of yellow which did little to flatter the natural pallor of his complexion. He was a little shorter than **Pride**, but not much for, being rather plump, his roundness made him seem shorter than he was. **Quickly**, the Adverb, who stood no higher than

Josh's waist, wore a loose-fitting multi-coloured tunic. He was here, there and everywhere, nimble and agile, weaving between the Verbs like an agitated sprite, ever ready to prod them into action. **Blind**, on the other hand, a quiet, thoughtful and slightly dishevelled figure wrapped in a bedraggled brown cloak, stood still, compensating for his lack of sight by listening attentively with his very large ears to all that was being said.

At this point, a new sombrely-dressed figure joined the debate. His serious, earnest expression indicated his chief characteristic - a dogged determination, which even those who disagreed with him had to admit enabled him to acquire an impressive grasp of almost any issue.

"It is not quite as simple as that," began the Verb **To Persist**. "If we examine this issue closely, we find that the Nouns are not in fact the powerful independent beings that **Pride** describes. They are certainly not indispensable and, it could be argued, they lack stamina. After all, even **Pride**, even he, must admit that the modest Personal Pronoun **He** can readily deputise for him."

He, a grey, rather non-descript creature, looked both pleased and embarrassed at the compliment which **To Persist** seemed to be paying him.

"In fact every Noun that ever there was," **To Persist** pressed on, "can be replaced by the over-worked and under-valued Pronouns. This demonstrates that no Noun is irreplaceable and it suggests to me at least that we would be unwise to entrust the leadership of our expedition to those who so readily delegate their responsibilities to other, lesser, citizens."

This clever double insult, directed at both the Nouns and Pronouns, provoked a growl of outrage from **Pride** but **To Persist** remained undeterred.

"We Verbs on the other hand do not depend on substitutes. When we are needed, we are there. And nothing else will do. Indeed, when it comes to issuing orders, both Nouns and Pronouns can be dispensed with altogether - as in the imperative "Be gone" - or the less polite formulation of the same exhortation, "Get lost". I might add that there is literally no end to our ability to get things done. Is that not why, when we verbs present ourselves in our preeminent form, as indeed I do now, we are titled 'the infinitive'."

Pride (who could no longer contain himself) interrupted **To**

Adventures in Grammarland

Persist who, being an infinitive, would otherwise, in all probability, have continued indefinitely. "Our use of Pronouns is evidence of our qualities of leadership, not a sign of weakness. Delegation is an essential tool of the successful commander. We Nouns have the good sense to save ourselves and our unique talents for those occasions when we are truly needed."

To Persist was about to resume his own line of reasoning when a colourful newcomer, with a permanently amused expression, joined the debate. **To Mock** wore what looked to Josh like an academic gown, with a red and white hood and a blue scarf.

"I sometimes wonder," said **To Mock** in a gentle, conciliatory tone, "whether we Verbs are not a little unkind and unfair to the Nouns. After all, there are Nouns whose usefulness is beyond dispute. Nouns like **Sun**, **Sea** and **Sky**; like **House**, **Hedge** and **Road**, those who represent things that genuinely exist - in short, the Concrete Nouns - are hard-working and reliable, if rather limited in their capacities. I'm sure we have no quarrel with them, nor they with us. They know their place," **To Mock** adjudged in a tone which somehow suggested that the place of such Nouns was well below that of the Verbs. He pulled his gown around him, giving the entirely false impression he had no more to say.

"No," **To Mock** continued after a pause, warming to his subject, "the cause for strife, it seems to me, arises from their more aristocratic, and might I say arrogant, brethren - the Abstract Nouns. Nouns like **Doubt**. They are for ever telling us of their importance; they claim pre-eminence. Yet some of us are unconvinced. Some of us, not me of course, but some less kind, have questioned the importance, the pre-eminence and, dare I say it, even the existence of some of these Abstract Nouns."

Now **Doubt** was widely noted for his general diffidence and lack of conviction but this questioning of his status, if not his very being, provoked an untypically robust response. "This is outrageous!" exploded **Doubt**, who at the mention of his name had rushed forward to stand beside his fellow Abstract Noun **Pride**. "You question the existence of those whose refinement and subtlety give them an obvious claim to superiority."

"Not I," replied **To Mock** gently, a wry smile playing around his thin-lipped mouth, "Not I, dear **Doubt**, but if I am honest, there are those amongst us, (no names, of course, and no pack-drill) who, for example, have their, dare I say it, doubts about one or two of your more refined brothers. **Truth** is a case in point. We hear so much of him - yet he is rarely, some say, never seen."

To Mock had touched a raw nerve and **Doubt** was taken aback. "It may be true", conceded **Doubt**, reverting to his more accustomed, less self-confident, role "that **Truth** is seldom seen. But that," he added rather sheepishly, "is because he likes to keep himself to himself."

Suddenly Syntax left Josh's side, bouncing forward. "Gentlemen, gentlemen, pray be silent for a moment - although I know it goes against the grain. Permit me to introduce," and here Syntax paused, perhaps for effect, perhaps because he was looking for the right description, "permit me to introduce," he repeated, " - a friend."

There was a murmur of curiosity. Syntax spun round towards Josh and hopped back to his side. "Come, boy, it is time to meet some of the citizens of Grammarland. Keep your glasses on; smile; and best foot forward."

6. The Oddest of Meetings

As Josh moved forward, the bolder Words crowded around him. "A boy," said **Rude**, a red-faced Adjective who spent much of his time quite happily in the company of Adverb **Gruffly** when they were not, as now, on opposite sides of an argument. "A mere boy."

"By what right," enquired **Pride** of Josh, "do you interrupt the private deliberations of this august gathering? You - an outsider, and a mere stripling at that. Pray tell me and my distinguished colleagues who and what you are?"

This was, of course, the same question Josh had asked of Syntax. Josh shot a glance at Syntax, hoping he might give some guidance on how best to deal with **Pride**'s aggressive questioning. But Syntax did not bat a silver eyelid; his only discernible response was to permit a hint of a smile to play around his finely engraved lips. **Pride** repeated his question with even greater insistence: "I said, who and what are you?"

Josh was beginning to dislike **Pride** intensely. He decided his best line of defence was attack. Taking a leaf out of Syntax's book, he replied: "You have in fact asked two questions. I will take them separately. As for who I am, I am Josh. And as for what I am, I am a boy."

"I see," said **Pride** gruffly. (The Adverb **Gruffly** had sidled over to stand beside **Pride** in the vague hope that, if a suitable Verb could be found, he might assist in the interloper's humiliation.) "The boy", **Pride** continued, now addressing the assembly, "has failed to answer my question according to the rules of Grammarland. His answers to my question tell us little or nothing."

"That is scarcely surprising," Josh countered, "since I do not see how I could be expected to know your rules or what kind of answers you expect. After all, Grammarland is not my land."

"Whether you are of this land or of some other is irrelevant. Are you not someone who has learned to speak, to write and to read? How can you possibly hope to succeed in your life, in this land or, indeed, any other, if you do not understand the rules which make all these things possible. You say you are a boy, that is to say, a Noun. You say you are Josh, that is to say a Proper Noun. Now, tell me, pray, what do 'boy' and 'Josh' mean?"

Josh groped for an answer but none was immediately forthcoming since he didn't understand the question. **Pride**, well-satisfied with the results of his ruthless cross-examination, addressed his fellow Words once more: "Gentlemen, I feel we should consider invoking the Curse of Er."

Josh had no idea what the Curse of Er entailed, but he certainly did not like the sound of it. "What is the Curse of Er?" Josh whispered to Syntax, but Syntax seemed lost in private meditation.

"'**Boy**', boy," said **Pride**, scenting his victim's fear, "is a Common Noun, common because it means 'any person of the male sex and of youthful age' - that is to say, any member of that group. 'Josh', however, is a Proper Noun, and Proper Nouns, as their name implies, are very particular. They refer to a specific instance which, in the case of 'Josh', is you."

Exasperation began to replace Josh's fear. 'My goodness,' he thought, 'I do hope the Words are not all going to be as boring as **Pride**.'

Pride, however, who loved the sound of his own voice, pursued his theme. "Of course," he continued, "your status would be somewhat elevated were you to dismiss the Indefinite Article **A** and call upon the assistance of the Definite Article **The**. Then,

Adventures in Grammarland

instead of being merely 'a boy', you would be 'the boy' - not any boy, but a particular boy. Rather more distinguished, eh? You might even be taken for '***the boy***' long honoured in Grammarland by the ancient lore of which the noble Syntax is custodian."

At this a sudden hush settled on the assembled Words, many of whom looked to Syntax for any indication that **Pride**'s speculation might be well-founded. Syntax failed to respond, his mind occupied elsewhere and his gaze fixed on the middle distance in an easterly direction. **Pride** took Syntax's failure to respond as confirmation that he could proceed with his prosecution.

"But, being merely 'a boy', your presence here is deeply offensive and, as the offence is grave, so should the punishment be harsh."

Josh determined to put a stop to **Pride**'s lecture. Not only was it tedious, but Josh felt somehow insulted and very concerned. He decided to try to turn the tables on his interrogator by asking some questions of his own. Plucking up his courage, he interrupted **Pride**, who was still in full flow. "Very well, **Pride**, tell me what does 'Pride' mean?"

Pride gave Josh a look of contempt. "What do you mean, what does 'Pride' mean?" Turning once more to his audience, he added, "The boy is, as I thought, a complete idiot. 'Pride'," he continued "is..."

For a moment Pride hesitated. "'Pride'," said **Pride**, "means 'Loftiness'." As he uttered this definition, to Josh's amazement, **Pride** floated gradually upwards, until he hovered some two metres above the assembly, his purple leather shoes with gold buckles dangling down over Josh's head. But Josh was undeterred, for his persecutor, despite his elevation, looked rather uncomfortable and slightly ridiculous. "I see," said Josh, "and what does 'Loftiness' mean?"

"What was that, boy?" **Pride** enquired, "I can't hear very well from up here. Speak up."

Some of the other Words began to snigger at **Pride**'s discomfiture. Josh was encouraged and repeated his question.

"'Dignity', boy, 'Dignity'," **Pride** replied, sinking slowly back to the ground with obvious, but short-lived, relief. Josh pressed on: "And what does 'Dignity' mean?"

"'Dignity' means 'Self-respect'," **Pride** declared.

Josh was on the point of admitting defeat but he decided to try just one more time. "And what does 'Self-respect' mean?"

"'Self-respect'," said **Pride**, preening himself in preparation for the devastating reply he felt sure he was about to deliver, "'Self-respect' means...," but here he trailed off.

Josh watched intrigued. **Pride** began to mumble and Josh could catch only some of what his erstwhile tormentor said - but certainly "'Arrogance', 'Haughtiness', 'Vanity', 'Vainglory', formed part of Pride's mutterings. Josh quickly realised that Pride was stumbling around, looking for a definition which would not detract from his own self-esteem. But, in his efforts to avoid one trap, he tripped into another. "'Self-respect'," he concluded in a tired voice, "is..., I mean, Self-respect means...'Pride'."

"Ah hah!" said Josh quickly, "so, at the end of the day, 'Pride' means 'Pride', rather like 'Josh' means me. The only difference is that you are merely one of a number of similar Words, whereas I am unique."

Josh's ploy had succeeded. **Pride**, who always comported himself with strict straight-backed military rectitude, now became completely rigid.

"Sometimes, **Pride**," Syntax intervened, in a tone that combined elements of anger and contempt, "sometimes you behave like a complete expletive. After this sorry performance, I am compelled to conclude that it is you, not this boy, who is deserving of the Curse of Er."

Pride was deeply offended. Despite his obvious military affiliations, the Abstract Noun appeared faint and, if the Adjective **Hurt** had not rushed forward to give **Pride** a degree of support, he might well have collapsed there and then.

"What is the Curse of Er?" whispered Josh to Syntax.

"Not now," said Syntax, impatiently. "It is not important. But understand this. You have already begun to explore the nature and some of the mysteries of Grammarland. Your questions bespeak intelligence, as well as wit and courage. These are the qualities for which you were chosen. But, you must ensure that your strengths do not become your weaknesses. Use your talents wisely, for even a rich man will become poor if he squanders his wealth. Always choose your questions well for true understanding lies as much in asking the right questions as in devising the right answers. And, one thing more, beware the fate of **Pride** for, as you have seen, **Pride** can be his own worst enemy."

His advice given, Syntax hopped into the middle of the group of Words and assumed an authoritative posture. "Listen to me". The hum of muttered comments subsided. "Listen to me", Syntax repeated. Dawn was breaking in Grammarland and the morning light suffused the now totally unfamiliar surroundings as far as Josh's bespectacled eyes could see. "We are gathered here to prepare for the Quest," Syntax continued. "Each and everyone of you will have to give of your best. For some, the trials and tribulations of the journey will be too great and, I tell you frankly, there will be casualties, even fatalities. Whether or not we succeed, I cannot predict. But this I know. Without the help of this boy, this mere boy, we are sure to fail."

While the gathered Words absorbed this blunt message, Josh took the opportunity to ask Syntax to explain what he meant by 'the quest'. Something told him that whatever 'the quest' was, there would be no way back, not, at least, until he had reached journey's end in this strange land.

"That is an apt question, but one I cannot answer," replied Syntax. "All I know is that the Quest is the reason you are here."

Josh fell silent. When he had walked through the Library door, he had left his own familiar world behind. As he had accompanied his guide into this strange new land, the Library itself had grown in size and then apparently faded away. He now seemed to be standing on an open plain, with grass-covered earth stretching for miles in all directions. To the north, he could see a range of mountains so high that the snow-capped tops were lost in the distant white clouds. To the east, lay open countryside, wide fields and rolling hills. Josh thought that he had best just wait and see.

"What is the Curse of Er?" he asked Syntax.

"That is a question I can and will answer," replied Syntax. "The Curse of Er is exile from Grammarland. Those who are so cursed are driven out across the southern tundra into the Desert of Inarticulacy which lies in the barren Wasteland of Hesitation. Such exiles are, as we say, "Lost for Words". Few, if any, return. Those who do are incapable of speech."

"You mean...?" said Josh, the question unfinished.

"Yes," said Syntax. "That's right. All they can say is "Er"".

7. Some Furry Friends

Josh looked at the gaudy assembly which had gathered at the edge of the trees as though uncertain whether to head out into the open countryside or to withdraw into the shady silence of the wood.

Each word wore whichever cloth and colour suited him. There were no discernible patterns of style although, despite their varied garb, there were distinct family resemblances between some of the Words. Indeed, it was obvious that many individual Adjectives were closely related to individual Adverbs. And even some Nouns bore striking resemblances to some of the Verbs. Josh made a mental note to ask Syntax why Words so closely related should be so argumentative, although he recalled that back in his own world people argued often enough. Even in his own family, his parents sometimes exchanged sharp words and, if Words were people here, it was not perhaps surprising that they too could be abrasive.

As Josh pondered this and many other questions, two furry creatures, one all white, the other all brown, locked together either in play or in fight, rolled across the short meadow grass towards his feet. "Whoops!" said the one that bumped into Josh.

"Excuse me," said the other, addressing himself to his companion. "'Excuse me', not 'whoops'".

"Hello," said Josh, who liked the look of these newcomers. "Who are you?" Both replied together, so that Josh could hear neither. "One at a time," Josh laughed.

Now both waited politely for the other to speak. "Oh dear," said Josh who realised he might have a long wait for an answer. "Very well, who are you, O white furry one?"

"I am **And**," said the white one, "and this is my friend, **But**. I'm pretty easy going but my friend here, I have to say, is not - mainly because he is always coming up with objections. We are..." and here he paused, either to give the next word due emphasis or because he found it difficult to pronounce, "... Conjunctions."

"And so are we," said two more furry ones, one grey, the other black. "I am **When**," said the black one. "And I am **If**," said the other. "We too are good friends," added **When**, "but whereas I'm quite decisive, **If** here tends to be a bit unsure of himself."

And and **But** and **If** and **When** were about the size of small cats - and not unlike cats in appearance - friendly sociable creatures who were extremely polite when they were not being outrageously mischievous.

"Then tell me, **And**, what do you do?" asked Josh, eager to get to know the Conjunctions better.

"We join other Words together," said **And**.

"But not just Words, whole groups of Words," added **But**.

"And whole Sentences," added **And**. "We're experts in our field."

"But so are they," said **But**, eager to involve **If** and **When** in the conversation.

"When we think it is right to do so," offered **When**.

"If it seems like a good idea at the time," chirped **If**.

Syntax, who still stood at Josh's side, interrupted. "Enough," he declared good-humouredly. "**And** and **But** and **If** and **When** will chatter away, playing and arguing, for hours. Wherever Words gather together you will find them. Simple, playful little animals they may seem, but do not underestimate them. **When**, for example, can perform the duties of an Adverb, or even those of a Pronoun or Noun, if called upon to do so. Be assured they and their friends will be of value to us before the Quest is over."

8. Syntax Takes Control

Meanwhile, the assembly waited attentively for Syntax to explain further the nature and purpose of the Quest.

"Now is the time," said Syntax to Josh "for us to organise the expedition. I will do my part. You must do yours." With that, Syntax hopped away from Josh into the milling crowd of Words, bouncing his way to a rise in the ground which gave him a good overview of the assembly. As soon as he had taken up this position, he coughed and then spoke in a silver-clear voice that carried well through the bright morning air.

"Noble Words, noble, one and all." The crowd fell silent. Evidently, Syntax was generally respected by the parts of speech, both high and low. "Noble Words, as you gather here to plan the Quest, we all know that there will be many arguments on who shall lead and who shall follow. Nouns will argue with Verbs. Adjectives will side with Nouns; Adverbs with Verbs. And other parts of speech will be forced to take sides. Or will wander off to talk amongst themselves - bored by the whole proceeding. But I tell you, if the Quest is to succeed, all Words must work together. Even then, our chances of success will remain slim. Because I know this is so, I wish to tell you a story."

Although Josh did not realise it at the time, Syntax had been very clever. If there was one thing that could silence a group of chattering Words, it was a good yarn. And Syntax's tales of the old days, when Grammarland had been governed by a real King and Queen and a noble court, were always immensely popular. Everyone settled down.

"An excellent idea," said several Nouns in chorus.

"Pray proceed," added an equal number of Verbs.

9. "The Great Conflagration"

"Once upon a time," said Syntax "a very long time ago, a King and Queen reigned in Grammarland. Although the King and Queen often argued with each other, under their governance there was peace and harmony amongst all the citizens of the Kingdom for many years - until one day the Queen made what seemed an innocent enough remark.

"My liege Lord," she said, addressing her husband in the traditional form, "Autumn is with us and the cold dark days of winter fast approach. Is it not now time for us to quickly take ourselves to our Southern Palace? I only wish that you had agreed to our departure from this damp Northern Castle some weeks ago."

Now, had the King been in a better mood, he might have let the matter pass. But he was not in a better mood, not even in a moderately good one, for, after so many years as ruler, the affairs of Grammarland were beginning to weigh heavily upon him.

"I might be able to tolerate a Split Infinitive," he said tartly. "Or even a Misplaced Only. But not both in one Sentence."

The many courtiers who served the royal couple, familiar with their frequent altercations, realised that they were about to witness a truly regal row. The Lord High Chancellor, a man much respected for his wisdom and impartiality, made as if to intervene, but the King's dark *brow made him think better of it. The Queen responded to her husband's rebuke quietly and, apparently, sweetly. But those who knew her well (in whose number we must surely count the King) understood that, when she used such a tone, she was at her most dangerous.*

"My Lord, it was not one Sentence but, if memory serves me right, two. If I have mildly transgressed against any of the more obscure edicts of the Kingdom, forgive me. Sometimes I find it just a little difficult to distinguish between a slavish subservience to the ancient rules of speech and outright pedantry. Whatever the case may be, please overlook my peccadilloes on this occasion and vouchsafe me an answer to my question. When may we leave?"

*Now the King was not at all amused by the Queen's reply. In fact, her answer simply served to convert his irritation into anger. Very well, he thought, she must be taught a lesson. "Bring me the Adverb **Quickly**" he commanded.*

***Quickly** was brought before the King. "Did you or did you not," asked the King in his most intimidating manner, "split an infinitive, to be precise the infinitive To Take?"*

*"Yes, your Majesty," replied **Quickly**.*

At this point, Selima, only child of the King and Queen, and, unusually, the court jester, decided it was time to make a contribution. "It's an exceptional rule, my Liege, that has no exceptions. Indeed, we might say that a rule without exceptions is an exception to the rule. Surely the King of Grammarland, endowed with such exceptional wisdom and

Adventures in Grammarland

power, would not forbid all exceptions - for such a ruling might inadvertently be applied to its author, who is manifestly so exceptional in every way?"

As the Lord High Chancellor had remarked on Selima's appointment, it was without precedent for a court jester to be so young, so female, so pretty and so royal but, from her earliest years, Princess Selima had shown a ready wit and, dare I say it, on occasions, wicked sense of humour. Furthermore, although no court is complete without a court jester, and although the rewards for such a position are always generous, there were few contenders in the court of Grammarland for the job. Both the King and the Queen had fearsome tempers and any jester who could not appeal as a last resort to familial ties ran the risk of an abrupt termination of employment, if not life. So it was that Selima, who from her earliest years had been determined to assert the rights of the female sex to equality, had on her eighteenth birthday demanded the vacant post as her birthday present. The King had been reluctant to comply with his daughter's demand but Selima had her mother's support and it is an unwise man who takes a stand against both his wife and daughter. By general consent, from that day, Selima had performed the role perfectly. The only dissenting voice was that of the Lord High Chancellor who found the girl's wit disconcerting and her role as court jester, given her female sex and her royal blood, peculiarly inappropriate.

*In normal circumstances, the King would have been mollified by Selima's wit and flattery for he loved his daughter deeply - but these were not normal times. In any case, the King had for some time harboured suspicions that his daughter secretly inclined towards the Queen's more liberal views. On this occasion, he frowned a paternal warning to his jester and proceeded with his cross-examination of the hapless **Quickly**.*

"Is the splitting of an infinitive against the rules of Grammarland or is it not?"

"Yes, your Majesty."

*The King turned from the quaking, shaking and manifestly contrite **Quickly** and called for the next offender.*

*"Bring me the Adverb **Only**," he demanded.*

***Only**, as ever a lonely and uncertain figure, was dragged forward, a truly pitiable sight.*

"Did you or did you not," demanded the King, "take up the wrong position in the Queen's speech? "Did the Queen not say "I only wish" when she clearly meant 'I wish only'. In short, did you not misplace

*yourself? How many times do I have to remind you and your fellow adverbs **Even**, **Merely**, **Really** and **Truly**, that the sense of a sentence so often depends crucially on the position you occupy? So why do you persist in ignoring my royal edict?"*

*I don't know. I don't remember," said the pathetic defendant. The misplaced **Only** was so terrified he could scarcely speak.*

"For goodness sake," exploded the King "Pull yourself together, man. Let me refresh your memory. The Queen said;

"I only wish that you had agreed to our departure from this damp Northern Castle some weeks ago."

Clearly what she meant to say was;

"I wish only that you had agreed to our departure from this damp Northern Castle some weeks ago."

Well, yes or no? Answer me. Were you not out of order?"

*The misplaced **Only**, shaking with fear, managed to control himself sufficiently to nod his assent.*

"Very well," continued the King, satisfied by the results of his interrogation. "We have before us two offending expressions. Before I pass sentence, have you anything to say in your defence.

"My Lord," said the Queen, "I have something to say."

"Then speak," said the King roughly, "but keep to the point."

"So sharp, my royal master?" Selima intervened again. "Then let us hope the point will prick, quickening sense into good sense."

"Hold your tongue," retorted the King, in a profoundly ill-humour. "You may be flesh of my flesh but, even so, when one has an itch one needs to scratch it, when one has a blackhead one may squeeze it, when one has a boil one must lance it. Lancing is the only pricking you are likely to see today. Another word, my dear daughter, and I shall have to decide whether scratching, squeezing or lancing is called for."

Given the King's love for his daughter, this was an extraordinary outburst which suggested to some of the courtiers that the King had become somewhat unbalanced. The Queen, however, remained entirely undaunted. The King's savage rebuke of their daughter made her even more determined to defy her husband. She rose from her throne and, as though to mock the King's justice, mimicked the mannerisms of a defending lawyer by inserting both her thumbs in the pockets of a non-existent waistcoat. Her posturing raised a titter in the court, silenced by the sight of a blood-vessel throbbing in the King's forehead, always a sign of impending royal rage. Undeterred, the Queen began;

"My Liege, my Lords, Ladies and Gentlemen, I cannot deny that the

Adventures in Grammarland

ancient rules of Grammarland have been transgressed. All of us, both high and low, will recall the lessons we learned as children. But now let me ask you to use your intelligence, as well as your memories." As she spoke the word 'intelligence', the Queen looked pointedly at the King. "Why were the ancient rules of Grammarland established? Was it not to enable us to express our thoughts clearly? Of course it was."

Selima, uncowed by the King's last rebuke or by the threat which had accompanied it, spoke up again. "Surely, it is simply a matter of having a clear mind, but, on this occasion, for such minor transgressions, can we not all agree to say, No Matter? Or, perhaps better, Never Mind. Or better still, Never Mind, it's No Matter. 'Though without mind and matter, might we not find ourselves in a non-existent pickle?" Selima was desperately trying to divert the King away from a bitter confrontation but by now it was clear to all that the King was in no mood for levity.

"Madam," barked the Monarch of Grammarland, addressing the Queen. "We do not need a lesson from you on the origins of the Kingdom's rules. If you wish to defend the accused, do so. But make haste for I fear, as we grow older, that my ability to listen, great though it is, has failed to keep pace with the expansion in your capacity to talk."

Many times the Court had witnessed tiffs between the royal couple. But always they had been conducted with at least an element of good-humour. On this occasion, the argument was becoming all too personal and all too serious. Even Selima had to admit that matters had gone beyond repair by any quip or joke.

*"The purpose of the rules of which you and I are custodians," replied the Queen, with a coldness of tone that confirmed the Court's worst fears, "is to enable us to express our thoughts clearly. If Adverb **Quickly** and the misplaced **Only** are to be punished, it must be because they obscured my thought. I therefore conclude there is no case to answer."*

"And how, madam, do you reach that conclusion?" asked the King, falling into the trap which his consort had laid.

*"Why, very simply," replied the Queen, condescendingly. "The fact that you found it so easy to determine what I meant, despite my transgression of the rules, proves that there was no offence. When correcting the misplaced **Only**, did you not yourself say 'Clearly what she meant to say...' If what I meant to say was 'clear', how have these Words offended? Only a Pedant would pursue the matter further."*

The Queen's argument seemed sound to many who listened, espe-

cially those (and there were many) who found the burden of conforming to all the rules and regulations of Grammarland somewhat onerous.

"By the Great Primer of our Fathers!" the King swore, using what was at that time the most powerful oath in Grammarland, "You preach sedition, Madam. When the archer fires his arrow at the target, we all know that he aims for the bull. But are we to draw no distinction between the arrow that hits the target and the one that misses? When the careless surgeon operates and the knife slips is he to be excused his professional incompetence on the grounds that it was clearly his intention to save the patient, not to kill him? What you meant to say may have been clear to the discerning and perceptive listener, but that does not exonerate you from the guilt of obscuring your meaning by sloppy use of language."

At this point, the Lord High Chancellor of Grammarland, now seriously alarmed by the direction of the argument, intervened. "Your Majesties" he began in a brave effort to placate the royal couple, "Can we not find common ground?"

"Common ground," snorted the King. "Certainly, and for the Queen, I suggest the commoner the ground the better. I have no doubt, as she slides from grammatical solecism to total inarticulacy, she will be trying to extol the virtues of grunts before we are through."

"My Lord," replied the Chancellor quickly, preventing the Queen from responding to the King's insult, "You are right to defend the rules *of the Kingdom. But, equally, we must not stifle the freedom of expression which gives life to our language. And we must accept that even the rules of Grammarland can be modified over time by usage."*

"The King," said the Queen, determined to make her point, "takes little interest in freedom, except his own, and as for nurturing the life in language, he nurtures as the fox nurtures chickens, as the spider nurtures the fly or, perhaps most appropriately in the present circumstances, as the executioner nurtures the condemned man."

"Enough!" said the King. "My patience is exhausted. I will not deny, Lord High Chancellor, that rules can change over time. But that does not in any way justify us in excusing individual deviations from the rules which pertain today. Nor shall we ever countenance, as it seems the Queen would wish, statements which do not mean what the speaker intended. My Lady," he now addressed his consort, "you wish to depart for the Southern Palace. Then go. And take with you all those in this court who find your views appealing. We", and here he used the royal 'we', "shall stay here for the present."

There was a stunned silence. The King and Queen, despite their past differences, had never been separated from the day of their wedding. The Lord High Chancellor spoke. "My Liege, is there not a way in which we can resolve this dispute."

"Or perhaps dispute this resolve," offered Selima, who was also, in her own way, desperately hoping to reduce the tension between her parents.

The King remained unmoved. The Queen spoke. "The differences that you suggest we resolve go to the very heart of Grammarland. I, and I know I speak for many, am weary of the arbitrary rule of the King, my husband. It will be a welcome relief to sojourn in the Southern Palace, free of restrictions. And this I promise those who join me. Freedom of expression shall be the order of the day."

"Chancellor," said the King, the vein in his forehead now throbbing rhythmically, "the dispute, as you call it, is ended. Madam, prepare yourself and your entourage - and leave at once. I am sure you will find my punishment of the Adverb **Quickly** and the misplaced **Only** - distasteful."

"My Lord," snapped the Queen, now openly defiant. "I shall obey but, mark my words, there shall be no punishing. Both the defendants were doing my bidding when they committed the offences with which you charge them. They are under my protection and shall join me on my journey south for it is clear they will only be safe with me."

"Already the rot spreads," cried the King. "So they will 'only be safe with you' - they will not be happy, they will not be free, they will not be fulfilled - merely safe. Take heed, all those who plan to follow the Queen. All she can offer is vagueness and confusion, with no hope of happiness, freedom or fulfilment."

"That is not what I said," shouted the Queen angrily.

"It is precisely what you said," the King replied, heavily emphasising the word 'precisely'. "So now the proven offender challenges the judgement and authority of the realm."

"This way disaster lies," said the Lord High Chancellor. "The strength of Grammarland lies in its unity."

"And that unity," the King interrupted, "depends upon respect for the law. Those who undermine the law, destroy that unity. Freedom, true freedom of expression, exists only within a framework of law. Those who see no harm today in minor transgressions will tomorrow find it easy to excuse far graver crimes against the state and, in the end, Ignorance will rule within this land. Madam, you will leave - and the offending Words will face their punishment. Or, if you persist, you shall be punished in their place."

What happened next, happened quickly, so quickly that to this day no one can be certain of the sequence of events. Both King and Queen had been schooled in the ancient magic arts.

The King, with the slightest movement of the little finger of his right hand cast a spell at the Queen intended to turn her, at least temporarily, into a small silver figurine, no more than a foot high. "Thus," thought the King, "she will be cut down to size, a shining example of the fact that those who diminish the rules of the Kingdom, diminish themselves."

The Queen, despite her praise of freedom and creativity, showed rather less imagination, simply calling on the faerie forces to turn her husband into a wooden stick, perhaps as a symbol of the strict discipline with which he ruled the Kingdom.

Which spell would have taken first, we shall never know, because the Lord High Chancellor and Selima, court jester and loving daughter of both her parents, aware that the actions of the royal couple endangered the whole realm, stepped forward to protest. In the event, both, seeking reconciliation and abhorring violence, bore the full brunt of this wild and errant sorcery.

When such powerful magic is abroad, onlookers must hope that the spells find their target for, when they go awry, none can foretell what damage will be wrought. On this occasion, two puissant spells collided, each thus failing to reach its goal. The energy released was indescrib-

able. Suffice it to say that within minutes the Northern Castle lay in ruins. Those who were able-bodied and quick-witted fled. Most of those who stayed perished in a swirl of arbitrary and undirected magic. Both the King and Queen vanished, sucked into a vortex of swirling light which carried them out through the highest window in the central turret of the Northern Castle and up into the cold grey sky like two autumn leaves. They were never seen again.

As for the Lord High Chancellor and Selima, caught in the eye of this abominable storm, it is believed that they survived, but only to see the disintegration of Grammarland. Word stood against Word. The Rules of Grammarland were broken and destroyed. And, as the King had predicted, Ignorance was to rule the land.

10. More About Grammarland

Syntax paused, his story at an end. He awaited the inevitable questions. Josh could see that the Words were deeply moved. Syntax had, for a brief moment, dispersed the mist of forgetfulness which obscured the time of long ago and had given the Words a glimpse of their ancient heritage.

"Will there ever be peace and justice again in Grammarland?" asked the Abstract Noun **Hope**, his bright eyes filled with tears of longing.

"It is easier to know the past than the future," replied Syntax evasively.

"It is far from easy to know the past," said **Doubt**, who generally found it difficult to believe anything he was told and most of what he saw. "How is it, Syntax, that you alone know so much of our past?"

"Why is it," cut in the Verb **To Challenge**, "that, whenever we gather together to discuss any matter, there is always a Noun eager to provoke an argument?"

"I was not provoking an argument," returned **Doubt**, "I simply was asking a question?"

"Enough," said **Forethought**, an Abstract Noun well-respected by all his fellow citizens. "**Doubt**, pray be silent. We have weighty matters to consider and a great Quest before us. Let us all be grateful for the help and advice which Syntax can give us." **Forethought** then addressed himself to Syntax. "We have listened attentively to your story of the ancient times but I fear that some here will not fully understand its significance. Will you, with your skill in such matters, enlighten them?"

Now Josh could tell that **Forethought** himself had not entirely grasped the point of Syntax's tale. But he was loath to admit it. 'You are right,' said a voice in Josh's ear.

"Who said that?" Josh blurted out. Of all his experiences so far in Grammarland, this was the strangest. The voice he had heard had not come from anywhere. It had been within his head.

'It was I,' said the same voice which Josh now recognised as that of Syntax. 'I should have warned you. You and I can communicate without speaking. It is one of the weapons we will have in our armoury when we set out on the Quest. It means that I can be honest with you without alarming the army of Words or betraying our thoughts to our enemies. Now, as I was saying, or rather thinking, to you, you are right. None of the Words fully understands the meaning of my story, although I hope and believe they have some glimmering of its import. You will quickly discover, as you journey through Grammarland, that individual Words, on their own, are not very bright.'

'How can I hear you when you are not speaking?' enquired Josh, still amazed by this novel experience. 'And how can you hear me? And why do none of the Words notice? Surely they can see that you are not paying any attention to them while you are communicating with me?'

'You ask so many questions, Josh,' said Syntax, 'and all I can do is seek for answers in half-forgotten memories of long ago. When I was very young, a mere sapling so to speak, we were taught that the soul of a Word was the meaning it bore. When the souls of Words gathered together, it was possible, not certain, mark you, but possible, that they would give birth to a thought. Once a thought was born, it had a life of its own; it existed. Not as in your world, where a thought stays in the thinker's head until the thinker uses Words to convey it, but as an independent entity - a Thought, if you like, in its own right. If someone had a Thought and wished to pass it to another, the Thought itself set out from the sender and arrived with the receiver at the speed, well, at the speed of Thought. It came to be called telepathy and I believe there are still vestiges of this phenomenon in your world. Of course, the art of sending and receiving Thoughts was lost in Grammarland after the Great Conflagration that consumed the Northern Castle. And nowadays, the Words spend so much time bickering that it is most unlikely that a new Thought will ever be born, never mind transmitted.'

'Then how is it that you and I can pass thoughts?' asked Josh.

'Because I have memories of the old world,' replied Syntax, 'and you are from the other world. Between us, if we are lucky, there will grow a bond that will restore Grammarland to its former glories.'

'And why do none of the Words notice what we are doing?' persisted Josh, although he only half understood the answer that Syntax had already given him.

'I told you that here time is not as uncompromising as in your world. In Grammarland, time stands still when nothing happens. The Words see nothing happening so, for them, no time has passed since we started this conversation.'

'I see,' thought Josh, but Syntax knew he didn't.

11. Preparations

"You asked me to explain the significance of my tale," said Syntax, addressing the vast assembly of Words, "and I will do so. But if, in the explaining, I give offence to any Word, I ask now that you will forgive me. It will not be my intention to offend, rather to tell the truth and to give us all a chance of success in the Quest."

"Grammarland was founded on certain principles. The rules by which the Kingdom was governed depended for their authority on those principles. When the King and Queen fought each other, they betrayed those principles. And they destroyed the Kingdom, allowing Ignorance to invade and conquer.

"Our Quest is to find those principles once more and to re-establish them throughout Grammarland. If we are to succeed, then all Words must work together. All Words must learn two things. First that no one word is more important than another."

Syntax continued despite the uproar engendered by this remark which seemed innocuous enough to Josh. "Secondly," Syntax persisted above the noise, "all Words must understand that, working together, we shall be far stronger than the sum of the strength of each word alone."

Once again, Josh intuitively knew that the Words did not

grasp the meaning of Syntax's second statement. And, still more strangely, he had the unmistakable feeling that Syntax himself did not fully understand what he had said.

'Yes,' said Syntax, using telepathy, 'You are right, boy. There is a mystery at the heart of Grammarland which even I can only partly know. That is why we need you.'

Syntax addressed the army of Words once more. "Prepare yourselves. When the sun is overhead, we shall set off."

Subdued by their inability to understand Syntax's meaning, yet excited by the prospect of action and the possibility of glory, the Words busied themselves with their preparations. Syntax and Josh observed them. After several minutes of close scrutiny, Josh asked; "Where are their weapons?"

"They have none," replied Syntax.

"Well it's not much of an army, if the soldiers are unarmed," commented Josh.

"We shall see," said Syntax, who seemed unwilling to discuss the matter further. "You, on the other hand, shall bear arms."

"I will?" responded Josh, surprised and not a little alarmed that he alone in the army should carry a weapon. "Courage, my friend," comforted Syntax. "There is little point in going on the Quest unless we are able to defend ourselves."

Before Josh could argue, Syntax performed a most extraordinary contortion. His silver head moved in an anti-clockwise direction, slowly at first and then more quickly, until it spun on its base.

"Don't be afraid," said the spinning head. "I am simply unscrewing myself." Syntax's silver head, now free of its thread, rose into the air, drawing with it a short blade which had been secreted inside the walking stick.

"There you are," said Syntax with evident satisfaction. "Not a mere walking stick after all - eh? Even in your world I held a secret unknown to you, and I suspect forgotten by your father and your father's father. Hold the blade carefully but firmly," ordered Syntax. Josh obeyed - and the silver head began to turn again until the blade itself was free. Syntax's head floated down on to the top of the empty stick, locked into the thread and, moving now in a clockwise direction, resumed its former position on the wooden body.

"There," said Syntax, fully restored, although somewhat

lighter. "Now, hold the blade away from you and press the button which you will find in the base."

Josh followed Syntax's instructions. When he pressed the button, two side pieces popped out, converting the blade into a sword.

Josh looked at his weapon, which was both dull and blunt, and was frankly unimpressed.

"The sword may not be the finest weapon in our world," conceded Syntax. "But it will nevertheless stand you in good stead - if you learn how to use it well."

"I suppose it's better than nothing," said Josh, still unconvinced, as he hung the sword on the dressing-gown belt at his side.

12. The Quest Begins

The sun was shining in an azure sky as the army of Words, with Syntax and Josh at its head, set off on the Quest, leaving the woods where no birds sang behind them.

"We shall head east, towards the ruins of the Northern Castle," Syntax had announced to the army. Telepathically, he had confided in Josh that he had no idea where to lead the army but the scene of the downfall of the Golden Age seemed as good a place as any. He had ended his thought-message with what was evidently a Grammarland aphorism: "If you wish to direct some sense into an army of words, you cannot succeed without a sense of direction."

The army was in high spirits as it tumbled across the open fields, leaving a broad swathe of well-trodden grass as they passed. Nouns and Verbs vied with each other in proclaiming the feats of glory they intended to perform, with the Verbs generally having the edge in expressing themselves - and the Adjectives and Adverbs joining in enthusiastically on one side or the other.

Pride, as ever full of himself, summoned the assistance of the Adjective **Brave** in his superlative form and announced; "I shall prove myself the Bravest."

"Without a **Doubt**?" enquired **To Mock**, hoping to stir up trouble between the Nouns themselves if he could. Despite his irritation, **Pride** decided to treat this remark with contempt. "May I suggest that the Noun **Fall** speaks next," continued **To Mock**, determined to cause mischief and merriment if at all possible, "since, in my experience, that is the normal sequence of events."

This sally produced widespread amusement but **Pride** was not to be so easily subdued. "We shall need more than wit when the battle begins," he retorted haughtily. "We shall need **Courage**," he concluded, once again emphasizing the value of Abstract Nouns and at the same time implying that **To Mock** might be in need of **Courage** when the time came.

"We shall need both," interrupted Syntax. "Indeed, we shall need all of you, working together in the community of Words."

The banter continued, but good humour prevailed for Syntax had succeeded in engendering a spirit of camaraderie.

ooo

Josh's head was buzzing with thoughts as he marched. What on earth was he doing in this strange land, leading an army of Words, with a sword hanging at his side? He looked down at his dressing gown and noticed that it had changed in texture. It now seemed to have the cut of a military tunic and the cord on which he had hung the sword was of leather. "Well," thought Josh, "in a land where walking sticks can speak and Words are people, and Thoughts can silently nip across space, why should I be surprised that a cord of cloth can turn to leather."

"There are more things in this world of ours," said a croaking, ancient voice, "than any one man can know."

Josh turned towards the source of the voice and saw an extremely ancient being, leaning on the arm of a much younger Word. "I am **Forswunk**," said the ancient one "and I have seen much in my life, young fella' me lad. I am not a well-educated person. I am no scholar. Those who work with their hands from the cradle to the grave have little time for books and high-fallutin' matters - but I have used my eyes and ears which is not a bad way to learn. And this much I know....."

Forswunk failed to complete his sentence, apparently overwhelmed by fatigue.

"**Forswunk** is a very strange name," said Josh addressing himself to **Forswunk**'s companion, who looked almost as tired as his ancient companion, but was, at least, less laden with years.

"I am the Adjective **Exhausted**," replied the younger one, "and I am also a past participle of a Verb, but I don't have the strength to explain that to you now. What I can tell you, however, is that neither **Forswunk** nor I am much looking forward to this Quest. It is sure to involve a long and arduous journey. As for the ancient **Forswunk**, a forebear in a sense of mine, but only in a sense, who means as much to me as I to him, so to speak, well frankly, I don't think he's up to it."

Josh looked from one to the other and had to agree that neither was cast in the heroic mould. But he was not downcast because, behind him, he could see a mighty army of excited Words and the vast majority seemed full of energy and confidence.

ααα

Josh's musings were interrupted by a soft melodious, though rather muffled, voice of a young girl.

> "Never so many
> and all so charming;
> armed to the teeth
> yet all so disarming
>
> Great feats predicted
> all so conceited;
> best foot forward
> till we're defeated."

"Who said that?" asked an astonished Josh.

"You said 'that'," answered the same melodious voice. "If you do not listen to yourself, Josh, how can you expect others to pay attention?"

It was by now evident that the voice came from the pocket of his tunic. "Well," thought Josh, "why shouldn't a garment speak? Everything else does."

"We might well be able to conduct a more civilised conversation," said the voice, "if I had a little more fresh air. I am very fond of fresh air. I am at my best, or so I'm told, when full of the stuff."

Josh patted the pocket of his tunic gingerly and felt a hard shape within. He slipped his hand inside and pulled out his flute. 'Of course!' Josh remembered, 'I brought the flute with me to help me to return to my own world.'

"That's better," said the flute. "There's nothing like a good breathful. By the way," she added, "it must surely be time I formally introduced myself. After all, you have spent hours holding me aloft, with, how shall I put it," she said coyly, "your lips pressed close to mine. My name is Melisa."

Josh no longer felt inclined to express amazement at the marvels of Grammarland. Instead, he asked; "What was that song you were singing?"

"That," said Melisa, "is the traditional marching song of the Words."

"It sounds rather pessimistic," responded Josh.

"Nonsense," said she dismissively.

"Well it sounded rather as though you were suggesting we would fail."

"I was," retorted Melisa. "I didn't mean your interpretation was nonsense. I meant the song was nonsense."

"Do you mean," persisted Josh, who was rather shocked by the flute's negative attitude, "that the marching song of the Words is nonsense?"

"I mean all marching songs are nonsense. They tell of heroic feats, of glory and of conquest. But that is not the stuff of which wars are made. Wars are about fear and blood and sweat. And, at the end, in most cases, nothing has changed. They are senseless."

"But your song was not about heroic feats, glory or conquest. It was about the truth as you see it. So why is it nonsense?"

"Because it is the truth only as I see it. And truth is commonly held to be only as strong as the number of those who assert it. In any case," said Melisa, changing tack, "if wars are senseless, it is entirely appropriate that any sensible song about them should be nonsense - or, as the venerable Syntax might say, 'Stuff and nonsense'."

"You know Syntax!" exclaimed Josh.

"Know him," laughed the flute, in a soft melodious fashion. "Oh, yes, I know him. I know him well - and I know him ill. In sickness and in health. Indeed, I know him better than he knows me."

Josh found Melisa's way of talking rather interesting. The flute was so full of surprises that Josh had no idea what she was going to say next.

"Why did you say that the Words were armed to the teeth?" asked Josh. "As far as I know, I'm the only one in the army who is carrying a weapon."

"How far is 'as far as you know'? If you know the limits of your knowledge, you must add that piece of knowledge to all the knowledge you know. But you will still have omitted your new knowledge of your new limits. Thus you will continue for ever adding to the sum of your knowledge without ever reaching a total."

"But that's silly," Josh replied. "I wouldn't really be adding to the sum of my knowledge."

"Very true," replied Melisa. "You would be adding up rather than adding to. It is however a wise man who knows the extent of his own ignorance. Know thine enemy. Is it better to know what you know or to know what you do not know?"

"You talk in riddles," said Josh, who was feeling frustrated by Melisa's habit of changing the subject. "No-one can know what they do not know because if they knew it..." - and here Josh paused for breath - "... then they wouldn't 'not know' it anymore."

"Aha!" Melisa returned, "but there is a difference between knowing you don't know something and not knowing there is something you don't know."

Josh paused for thought. "You mean the difference between not knowing how to speak German and, until today, not knowing about Grammarland. I knew I didn't know German but I didn't know I didn't know about Grammarland."

"You show promise," said the flute with a laugh. "Perhaps you were not such a foolish choice after all."

"You haven't answered my question," Josh was determined not to be distracted by the flute's antics. "About saying the Words were armed to the teeth," he reminded the voluble flute.

"Where else should Words be armed to?" replied Melisa, undeterred. "Certainly tongues and lips have a part to play, but teeth are worthy of the greatest respect. Tongues are for tasting and lips are for kissing - but teeth are the armoury of the mouth - and the mouth is the home and hearth of all Words, with only teeth to defend them."

"I give up," said Josh, exasperated.

"Don't give up," said Melisa, for the first time genuinely concerned. "Don't ever give up. That way disaster lies."

13. The Bog of Disuse

The army made good progress, travelling east. Gradually, the bright sunlight which they had enjoyed the day before faded. The sky turned a dull grey and a light drizzle began to fall, swathing the landscape in mist and making it difficult to see any great distance.

After about one hour, Josh noticed that the ground was becoming softer and the grass on which they marched a more luxuriant green. At each step, droplets of water leapt ahead of Josh's feet from the toes of his shoes. Syntax, with remarkable agility, continued to hop on, but it was clear to Josh that some of the Words, particularly the older ones, were having some difficulty in keeping pace. Josh caught up with Syntax.

"This will be the first test of our resolve," said Syntax, not waiting for Josh's question. "We are crossing the Bog of Disuse."

By now the earth was entirely sodden. Josh felt his feet sinking into the ground with a squelching noise. As he tried to lift his left foot, it felt as though a hidden hand had grasped it, holding it back. And when he put his weight on the right foot, in an effort to raise his left, the right foot sank too.

"Follow me," instructed Syntax. "There is a way through

the Bog. It is a narrow path in places and, unhappily, I am not entirely sure of its course, but I know we must continue. If we stay here, we shall all perish."

Josh looked back at the army of Words. No longer could he hear the proud boasts of glorious deeds. All were absorbed in trying to find ground solid enough to support their weight. The indefatigable Syntax hopped this way and that, probing with his base to find the safest route, and the Words now straggled out behind him in a long column as far as the eye could see.

Suddenly, there was a cry of fear and desperation from behind them. Josh turned and saw **Exhausted** gesticulating wildly. Josh ran back to find out the cause of the Adjective's alarm.

"I must save him," screamed the distraught **Exhausted**.

Josh, now by the side of the agitated Adjective, could see **Forswunk**, well off the path that Syntax had set, up to his waist in the Bog and slowly sinking.

Josh called out "Hold on!" and took a step towards the ancient one. But his own foot disappeared ominously into the hungry mud and it was only with the greatest difficulty that he managed to withdraw it to firmer ground.

"We must do something," said Josh to **Exhausted**.

"It's all my fault," said the Adjective. "I pushed him off the path. I didn't mean to. But the path was narrow. We were walking side by side. When there wasn't enough room, he just wandered off."

By now, the ancient **Forswunk** had sunk up to his chest. He raised a thin right arm as though to wave a sad farewell to his companions. He showed no signs of alarm, though Josh could see a look of sad despair in his weary eyes.

"There is nothing we can do," said Syntax in a firm and measured tone. Syntax had hopped back to Josh's side.

"But...," said Josh. And then, because he knew Syntax was right, he said no more.

"You have served us long and served us well," Syntax called to the head of **Forswunk**, which, apart from an upraised arm, was now all that showed above the surface of the bog. "Although many will forget you, I promise you a place forever in the Hall of Words."

The Bog tugged once more and the mud rose up to seal the eyes and ears that had seen and heard so much. The upraised hand, now the only visible sign of **Forswunk**'s whereabouts, slid slowly down until, with an almost imperceptible twitch, the fingertips finally disappeared. For a moment, there was a dip in the surface of the Bog. Then three large bubbles of air gradually extricated themselves from the mud, with a sticky, slurping noise - and it was over.

With **Forswunk**'s demise, Josh felt a cold thrill of fear. Dreadful things could happen in this strange and alien land. He was reluctant to discuss his alarm with Syntax. He knew Syntax would not approve and, in any case, he felt sure that Syntax sensed what he was thinking and feeling. As if to show that this was the case, Syntax turned to Josh. "There is no time to explain now. Later, perhaps. For the present I must concentrate my energies on finding safe passage for the rest of the army through this Bog."

ㅁㅁㅁ

After another mile of bogland, which it took them all day to cross, the ground became firmer at last. There were still patches of the brilliantly green vegetation, which Josh had discovered marked the most dangerous areas, but it was now easy to find solid ground.

"We will rest here for the night," announced Syntax.

14. Campfires

The Words made camp. Behind them, in the west, lay the Bog of Disuse. To the east, before dusk fell, Josh had seen a wide expanse of open fields broken in the middle distance by undulating hills. It seemed to Josh that he stood between a danger past and any number of unknown dangers yet to come in a strange world, full of uncertainties. But at least the ground beneath his feet was firm which, after the day's adventure, was a source of very considerable comfort.

That night the Concrete Nouns proved their worth to all. **Tent**, with the help of the auxiliary verb **To Be** and various adverbs, was here, there and everywhere, providing shelter for the foot-soldiers. Aided by the Verb **To Search**, the Nouns **Wood** and **Flint** persuaded **Fire** to ensure that the army was well protected against the cold night air.

Syntax, like the good general he was proving himself to be, spent several hours hopping amongst his troops, giving encouragement and comfort wherever it was needed. The mood in the camp was mixed. The first day of the Quest had taught all the Words that there would be no glory without danger and no victories without risk. Already, some of the weaker Words had been lost. And there were others in no condition to continue. Nevertheless, the vast majority remained in good heart, strengthened by the realisation that they had passed the first test.

"We have sustained few losses," said Syntax to Josh when he returned. "**Pilgarlic** and **To Fribble** are missing, although happily their relatives **Bald** and **To Stammer**, survived and they will have to do. We know the sad fate of the ancient **Forswunk**, and there were others of his age who suffered similarly. One or two of the older personal pronouns cannot go on. I have told **Thou** and **Thee** to remain here, at the edge of the Bog of Disuse. We will make do well enough with their more versatile brother **You**, though I must admit **You** lacks a little of their distinction."

The night was cold but it was not the chill air that made Josh shiver. He was unable to forget the expression of complete despair on **Forswunk**'s face as he had sunk forever into the Bog of Disuse. Syntax, aware of the boy's unhappiness, settled his base into a convenient hole in the ground beside Josh, and began one of his stories:

"Before Time began, which is a very long time ago, there was THE WORD. THE WORD meant nothing and yet It meant everything. THE WORD, you must understand, was not a Word. It had within It all possible Words.

"And THE WORD created NOUN and VERB and saw that it was good. And NOUN and VERB became flesh and from their union came all the Nouns and Verbs that people Grammarland. To the Nouns THE WORD said; 'Go forth and multiply', and the Nouns, created in the singular form, were enabled to be plural; and to the Verbs THE WORD said: 'I give you different forms so that, whether Nouns be singular or plural, you shall agree with them and there shall be peace and harmony between you; and you shall have tenses, past, present and future, so that you and, with your help, your fellow Words may move freely through time. And THE WORD created for the Nouns and Verbs, as their helpmeets, Adjectives, Articles, both Definite and Indefinite, and Adverbs, to walk with Noun and Verb, to aid and comfort them. And then THE WORD created creatures of the field. Conjunction and Preposition It created, to serve the children of Noun and Verb all the days of their life."

Josh listened attentively to Syntax. It helped to take his mind off the dreadful fate of **Forswunk**. And, besides, he was now convinced he needed to learn more about Grammarland, if he was to survive, let alone succeed in, the Quest. Syntax continued.

"And THE WORD knew that, with so many Words of so many different types, that there must be laws to govern their conduct. And THE WORD said: 'Let there be rules to govern the behaviour of each Word, so that all Words will know their place and their significance and will love their neighbours and will work with all other Words for the common good'."

"These are the rules of Grammarland, the rules which one day the King and Queen of Grammarland were to destroy in one stupid, senseless argument."

As Syntax recalled the destruction of the Golden Age, his eyes filled with silver tears - but he made a great effort to pull himself together, for the true purpose of his story-telling was to comfort Josh.

"THE WORD", he continued, *"which was wise beyond mere verbal description or mental comprehension, realised that for Words, as for all forms of life, there must be a birth, a growth, a maturity and a death. But THE WORD was not only wise; THE WORD was also merciful. And It decreed that, when Words reached the end of their lives, if they had worked well and stood for what is right according to the rules of Grammarland, they should pass into a final resting place, the Great Hall of Words, where their names would be listed forever as industrious citizens of Grammarland and honourable servants of THE WORD."*

"So you see, my boy," concluded Syntax, "Forswunk did not cease to exist when he fell into Disuse: he entered the Hall of Words, where all his works will be remembered until the end of time which, like going back to the beginning of time, is a very long time indeed."

"But will we ever see **Forswunk** again?" asked Josh, who did not find Syntax's story quite as comforting as its teller had hoped.

"No, we shall not see him again. But, although he is no longer with us, I wished you to know that he had not lived in vain nor is his name lost forever."

Josh had more questions to ask but, before he could speak, uproar broke out in the camp. A group of Words, gathered around one of the many glowing camp-fires, was fighting.

Josh could not see clearly who was involved. The light from

the fire was poor and, in any case, the brawling Words presented themselves as a tangled mass of arms and legs.

"That will be the Possessive Pronouns making trouble again," said Syntax.

A rather dishevelled-looking Word emerged from the melee. "That's **Mine**", shouted an agitated Noun, who promptly grabbed **Mine** by the scruff of the collar and pulled him back into the centre of the fight. No sooner had **Mine** entered the fray once more than another particularly aggressive Noun grabbed **Mine** and screamed; "No, that's **Mine**; this is **Yours**." **Yours**, like **Mine** a possessive pronoun, squared up to **Mine**, more than ready to fight. The object of the argument was some freshly cooked bread which had just been pulled from the embers of the fire. Several of the Words involved in the fracas were unfamiliar to Josh but he was able to identify the two Pronouns, **We** and **Me**, and a form of the Verb **To Fight**..

More Words gathered round. Most began to chant; "Fight, fight, fight" but the verb **To Forgive** refused to join in and **To Share** clearly also had reservations. As the non-combatant Words pressed forward to enjoy a better view of the brawl, a dispute broke out amongst the audience, threatening to provoke a whole series of scuffles.

"What shall we do?" asked Josh nervously. "We will lose half the army before we meet an enemy."

"Don't panic," said Syntax, as though this was a familiar and regular occurrence. "Take out your flute and play them some music."

Josh had not told Syntax that the flute was apparently a talking rather than a musical flute and now was not the time to confide in his mentor. Josh took out the flute and placed it to his lips. No sooner had he emitted a short breath than the most beautiful, soothing and honeyed music came forth. Since Josh had never been very successful at playing before, he gasped in amazement and took the flute from his lips.

"Your contribution to my attainments may be modest," said Melisa with a light, girlish, perhaps a little flirtatious, laugh. "But it is, nevertheless, necessary. If you don't blow, I can't play. Shall we continue?"

Josh returned the flute to his lips and blew once more. His

fingers moved up and down the keys with a dexterity they had never before possessed and the soft, gentle sounds soared up with the smoke from the dying fires into the black velvet of the night sky.

The effect on the battling Words was no less dramatic than the effect on Josh. All stopped fighting to listen to Melisa's mellifluous tones and those directly involved in the original argument, with the help of some of the onlookers, arranged themselves effortlessly into a coherent formation.

> *"Forgive Me.*
> *We, who Have Fought over a trifle,*
> *will Share the food.*
> *What's Mine is Yours."*

Syntax noted Josh's puzzlement and said: "Before you ask me a dozen questions (many of which I cannot answer), let me tell you what I know. Words have always responded well to music. It is widely believed that in the Golden Age every Word had a natural ear for melody. Many of the ancient stories tell how nothing gave the royal court greater pleasure than the joining of apt Words in song. Of course, with the Great Conflagration, that skill was almost entirely lost. But it is still true, as you have just witnessed, that music will calm the most obstreperous Word. You have done well, my boy. You have already shown signs of the POWER".

Syntax placed a peculiar emphasis on the word 'POWER', as though it had some special significance in Grammarland. Josh decided that it was time for honesty.

"Syntax, it wasn't me that made the music. I don't have any power."

"Then where did those sounds come from?" asked Syntax.

"From the flute," said Josh.

"Of course they came from the flute, but were you not the flute-player?"

"Not really," said Josh, determined to make matters clear.

For some time, Josh had felt a very real anxiety. Syntax, and indeed the whole army of Words, seemed to expect great things of him. He alone carried a weapon. He alone could communicate with Syntax without speaking. Now he was believed to be a gifted musician who possessed some magical power. But he was just an ordinary boy caught up in an extraordinary adventure.

"Not really," Josh repeated. "I blew and the flute played. You see, it's a rather unusual flute."

"Unusual," interjected Syntax, "unusual in what way?"

Josh thought to himself that a flute which could play without the aid of a flautist was in itself pretty unusual but he decided not to state the obvious. "Well, first of all, she talks."

Still Syntax failed to respond. He queried neither the claim that the flute could speak nor that it was of the female sex.

"And secondly she claims to know you."

"Well, well, well," said Syntax. "I wondered how much she had told you. Yes, the flute and I are old acquaintances. After all, we shared the Library in your world for a number of years. And yes, the flute can talk, though I should warn you that most of what she says is not worth the listening. It is not impossible, however, that she may be of some service."

Evidently Syntax had some doubts about Melisa's credentials and there was a mildly grudging tone in his voice when he conceded that the flute might be of use.

"Now listen to me, Josh," said Syntax in his most serious manner, "and listen carefully. What I am going to tell you now, I only half understand myself. If we are to succeed, we must find a way to re-establish the old order of Grammarland. This means, as I have said before, that all the Words must work together. In the Golden Age, there were three main ways of organising Words - Phrase, Clause and Sentence - and the greatest of these was the Sentence. It is, I must admit, a mystery to me but I have some glimmering of understanding. When words join together, they become stronger. As a good Sentence grows, the possibilities decrease until, by the end, there is no room for manoeuvre. And yet, somehow, at the very moment when the Words of a Sentence are completely trapped, at that very moment, they fulfil themselves. They become stronger, far stronger than the sum of their individual strengths. I know it is all very confusing. But that is because I do not really understand. And that is why you are here. For example, in the argument you have just settled (with or without the help of that garrulous flute), a number of Words were at each other's throats. When you calmed them, they came to their senses, so to speak:

Adventures in Grammarland

> *"Forgive Me.*
> *We, who Have Fought over a trifle,*
> *will Share the food.*
> *What's Mine is Yours."*

"Somehow, you persuaded all the Words directly involved in the fracas to form three Sentences. In the second Sentence, you made a Clause and, within that same Clause, a Phrase. That ability, to make sense out of chaos at any time, is the POWER, or at least as much of it as I can grasp. And that is why we need you and why, without you, we cannot succeed. Now, no more questions, please. Not because I do not have the patience but because I do not have the answers."

ααα

Josh settled down to sleep. It had been a long day and, despite his excitement and his anxieties, he was very tired.

"He really can be a boring old stick," said a voice from inside Josh's tunic. "It's odd that one of his composition should be unable to see the wood for the trees. He prattles on about a Clause like;

"who have fought over a trifle"

and entirely fails to see the joke lying curled up in the Phrase."

"What joke?" asked Josh, who was so sleepy that even Melisa's eccentric wit was unlikely to keep him awake much longer.

"Well, they said they were fighting 'over a trifle'. But they were actually disputing ownership of a piece of bread. Had the bread been a metaphorical slice, it would be anything but trifling, since symbolically bread tends to represent either the staff or the bread of life. On this occasion, it was indeed a trifling matter, since we were talking bread of the common flour, butter and water variety but it was not literally a trifle. If it had been a truly a trifle, the combatants would have found themselves in custard pie territory."

By now, Josh was fast asleep. "Never mind," said the flute. "Sleep well, young Josh, you have learned quite enough for one day. In any case, no joke is funny, if you have to explain it. Especially, when it's not much of a joke to start with!"

15. The Giant Oath

At dawn, the army of Words broke camp. It was a grey hazy morning, with the mist loitering about, resisting the weak efforts of the watery sun to disperse it.

Josh awoke to hear the clatter of an army preparing itself for a long march. The Verbs were particularly active in getting things done and the Adverb **Quickly** was much in evidence, speeding the efforts of now this Verb, and now that.

"How did you sleep?" asked Syntax.

"Very well," Josh replied. "And you?"

"Like a log," cut in Melisa quietly, so that only Josh could hear. "How else would you expect a stick to sleep?"

"Well enough," replied Syntax. "We will continue to march east, towards the ruins of the Northern Castle. Soon the sun will begin to clear the mist. It is time we set off, before the sun becomes too hot."

ooo

Before the morning mist had cleared and while the dew still lay heavy on the ground (a sombre reminder of the previous day's

Adventures in Grammarland

trials in the Bog of Disuse), the army was on the move. As they skirted a small hillock, Josh ran onto the higher ground and looked back. It was a strange but thrilling sight. Tens of thousands of Words were marching, moving across the plain like an undulating magic carpet of many colours. Nouns still tended to keep to themselves, as did the Verbs but, here and there, some mingled. Adjectives and Adverbs moved more freely, striking up conversations with each other. Josh noticed for the second time family resemblances between some of the Adjectives and Adverbs. The Adverb **Quickly** joined conversation with an Adjective which looked so similar that they could have been taken for brothers.

"I know," said Syntax, who had joined Josh on the mound to review his troops. "You and I can see it so clearly. Many of these Words are of the same family. Indeed, if the old stories of THE WORD are true (and who in Grammarland dares doubt it?), all the Words are part of the same great family. And yet," he added sadly, "at the least excuse, they fight each other."

As though to prove his point, the Adverb **Quickly**, half in play and half in earnest, attempted to trip the Adjective with whom he was talking. He failed and was unmistakably piqued by the Adjective's triumphant response. "You should know, dear friend, that I am too **Quick** for you."

Syntax and Josh rejoined the column, making their way to the front, in the company of the mildly chastened **Quickly**.

"If we succeed, will there be harmony amongst the Words, once the Quest is over?" Josh asked Syntax.

Before Syntax could answer, or avoid the question (which was more likely), a familiar piping voice came from inside Josh's pocket; "Once the Quest is *over* what, over where, over here or over there, or over the moon perhaps, like the athletic cow."

"I warned you about Melisa," Syntax remarked to Josh. "I fear she is having a brain-storm. On such occasions, the less heard of her the better. It's often as much as I can manage to keep her under control."

"As I was saying," interrupted Melisa, "over what or over where? After all, isn't **Over** a Preposition, and so shouldn't it go with something, just as **With** goes with something? I think, Syntax, you're **Up**, yes **Up** a gum tree, on this one."

Josh, while slightly alarmed by Melisa's provocative behaviour, could not hide a smile.

Syntax looked most put out by all this. "For your benefit," he said stiffly turning to Josh, "**Over** often fulfils a prepositional role but, when not engaged in prepositional activity, can also serve as an Adjective meaning 'finished' or 'completed', as in 'once the Quest is over'."

"Oh, I see," said Josh, "so some Words do more than one job. Isn't that a bit tiring?"

"No," replied Syntax, "lots of Words are _under_-employed and anyway have been trained from the beginning in multi-tasking. Of course we do have to watch against them being _over_-worked. You will have noticed that in what I have just said that **Over** and **Under** serve not as Prepositions, nor even as Adjectives, but as Adverbs, qualifying the Adjectives 'employed' and 'worked'. Yes, I must admit it can be a little confusing. Normally such Words can switch jobs without much difficulty - and even, in some instances, pray note, identities. Take **Report**, for example. Most of the time he is a rather academic fellow who occupies himself chronicling what's going on in rather elegant hand-writing. But then, all of a sudden, he becomes an entirely different personality, a loud, raucous chap, similar in sense to the noun **Bang**, who, like **Bang**, likes to be in the thick of the action." Syntax paused, having lost the thread of his argument.

Josh, not surprisingly, had not really followed all of this but he tried to look interested. Syntax recovered his composure: "A preposition, as I think I was saying, is a prop, it props up other Words. Let me see now. Ah yes, you over there, **Up**, come here. Don't just stand there idly", Syntax commanded. "Do something useful, prop something up other than that tree. You see what I mean," he said turning back to Josh, "about Words often being under-employed."

Up, who had set out quickly on the march, was now resting, languidly leaning against a tree. **Up** did not look pleased at being so peremptorily summoned by Syntax but he knew better than to disobey. As **Up** moved towards them he crossed the path of the possessive pronoun **Yours**, now fully recovered from the previous night's brawl, who happened to be marching past locked in an embrace with the Adverb **Truly**. **Up** halted their progress and tried to prize **Yours** loose but only succeeded in making him hold on even more tightly. This went on for some time.

Syntax stamped the ground impatiently. "For goodness sake,

Up, do stop that and find something else a little more proper to prop up."

"Tee hee!" Melisa giggled, "into a little word play, are we? Not really your bag, I would have thought. What's all this about proper, prop and preposition? Not much prepositioning and propping for **Up** in 'prop up', is there? I mean, **Up**'s out on a bit of a limb in 'find something a little more proper to prop up', isn't he? No propping up there, as far as I can see. As a matter of fact, **Up**'d fall off the end of the Sentence if he wasn't himself propped up by a full stop. And, as Syntax often says, **Up**'s not really up to wrapping up a Sentence. It's a case of **Up** getting above himself - or should that be ahead of himself?"

Melisa said all of this very quickly, indeed so quickly that even Syntax looked momentarily nonplussed and, before he could gather his wits, heard himself saying, to the accompaniment of Melisa's almost hysterical laughter, "That's enough, Melisa, what on earth do you think you're up to?"

Josh noticed that, in his disarray, Syntax had finished his last remark not just with one Preposition, but two. It crossed his mind to suggest that 'up to' was 'not on' as a way to end a sentence. But he thought better of it.

ooo

Marching gradually became more difficult and Josh realised that they were now making their way up an increasingly steep incline - so steep that the brow of the hill obscured the distant horizon.

"We may be lucky," said Syntax, "but I suspect we shall face our next test before we put this obstruction behind us."

Josh was about to seek more detailed information on the form the 'next test' might take, when a large round object began to rise above the brow of the hill, like a dark and threatening sun.

Josh stopped in his tracks. "Syntax, what is that?" he asked in amazement. The dark sun continued to rise until a complete head (for such it was) became visible. As the figure loomed higher and higher, a dreadful thumping sound vibrated through the ground. The entire army halted. Questioning murmurs and gasps of fear subsided, until all was silence, except for the thud, thud, thud.

By now, the shape of a mighty giant was starkly silhouetted

against the sun which had risen high in the east. He stood so tall that his head almost touched the scudding white clouds that flew across the bright blue of the morning sky.

"By Blunder, what in Gruber's name, are you niffing little padongas doing in my uberglubbing neck of the woods?" said a deep, gruff, booming voice that echoed back and forth across the surrounding hills, far above the heads of the assembly.

Josh looked towards Syntax but it was clear that Syntax expected Josh to reply.

"Hello," said Josh, nervously. "We are on a Quest." Josh felt that this answer was rather vague but, since he did not know any more himself, he thought it would have to do.

The giant grew still larger. "Well, by all the niffing Slabs of Snit, you can niffingwell turn round and scuff off - and take your pack of misky padongas with you." With this, the giant stamped his foot and the entire hillside seemed to shudder with fear. "Or I'll step on the whole niffing lot of you," he added for good measure.

Josh guessed that this was no idle threat, since the giant appeared to be quite capable of exterminating several hundred Words at a time with each step of his mighty boots. He was about to appeal to the giant's better nature (the existence of which he seriously doubted), when a voice from inside his tunic said; "He seems to do an awful lot of 'niffing'". Evidently, teasing Syntax had not exhausted Melisa's mischievous mood.

This remark struck Josh as quite funny. Indeed, he was so nervous that, when he thought about, it struck him as hysterically funny and he burst out laughing - a kind of raw, wild laugh.

"By Gruber and Snit, I'll rip your niffing entrails out of your misky little body," roared the giant. "What's so uber-niffing-funny, you erdy little grot?"

Through the tears of laughter that were running from his eyes, Josh noticed that, although the giant was extremely angry, he seemed to have become a little smaller. Not much smaller, but certainly he was now no bigger than when they had first met.

"I was just wondering," said Josh, encouraged by the giant's modest diminution, "I was just wondering why you do so much 'niffing'."

The giant was clearly taken aback by Josh's remark, so Josh decided that there was nothing to lose by pressing home his attack. "I mean it's not every day that I have the honour to meet the world's greatest Niffer," he added, with mock deference.

"That's the way," said Melisa.

"I'm not a Niffer, you fatulent little padonga, I am the Giant Oath. And no misky little erd is niffing-well going to talk to me like that."

For all his rage, it was now clear beyond a doubt that the giant was shrinking. And the angrier he became, the more he shrank.

"I'm not trying to upset you," Josh continued, "but I find it rather difficult to understand what you are saying. For example," and here he mimicked Syntax in one of his more pedagogic moments, "what is an 'erd' and, in particular, what is a 'misky' little 'erd'? I know what 'little' means and it is certainly true that, relative to you, I must appear rather small, though the difference in size is becoming less pronounced as time passes. But I am unclear as to the precise meaning of 'misky' and 'erd'."

The giant began to splutter and a jumble of strange words

poured forth. Whatever he said was entirely unintelligible, though Josh noted an abundance of 'niffs'.

"Do you mean," asked Josh helpfully, "that you have a low regard for me and my friends and that you would feel happier if we went back the way we came?"

By now the Giant Oath was no more than twice Josh's height. "If so," Josh persisted, "would it not be simpler to say what you mean, using words that we can all understand? You see, by the time we have removed from what you say all the words that don't mean anything, or which just tell us how angry you are, there's not much left."

For a moment, Josh thought he had gone too far, because Oath, who was now inexpressibly angry, began to grow again. But he need not have worried for the giant was not only growing upwards, he was also growing outwards: indeed he was growing in all directions. And as he grew, he somehow seemed to thin out, like an expanding balloon. He grew and grew until he stretched across the whole of the sky to the east - and then, with a deafening bang, he exploded.

For a minute, a light drizzle fell on the army of Words. And then it was over. The sky was as blue as ever and the sun, which had now risen high in the sky, shone down hotly, evaporating the last traces of the giant.

A cheer arose from the army of Words - and then a chant: "Josh, Josh, Josh", till the hills which had so short a while ago reverberated to the incomprehensible blathering of the Giant Oath, now echoed in triumph to the name of a small boy.

"You have done well," said Syntax, "but, before success goes to your head, let me tell you that the Giant Oath was the easiest of the trials we must face."

16. Misuse

Josh felt extremely proud of his victory over the Giant Oath but he was honest enough to know that he owed his success in large measure to Melisa.

"Thanks for the tip," said Josh to Melisa, when he knew no-one else could hear him.

"It was nothing," replied Melisa graciously. "I'm an expert on all kinds of wind movements, including sudden effusions of hot air. And always remember, however small the pin, it will burst the biggest balloon," Melisa added lightly. "You could say it's the point of the pin that's the point of the pin, if you see my point."

"Had you met the Giant Oath before?" asked Josh.

"No, but I have often heard stories about him. He is able to terrify those who are faint-hearted. But he is just hot air - all wind, signifying nothing. You will invariably find that those who swear a great deal have spent some time in the tundra that borders the Desert of Inarticulacy and, although they have narrowly avoided the Curse of Er, they find it difficult to express themselves. In fact, they're rather pathetic and, if they weren't so often aggressive (a direct result of their inability to communicate), I could pity them."

Melisa fell silent. It was obvious that Melisa, who took such delight in verbal gymnastics, found the Giant Oath and his kind a rather tedious subject for conversation.

ooo

Josh rejoined Syntax at the head of the army and they marched on in silence for several miles. The landscape was pleasant enough, rolling meadows heightened here and there by gently rising hills. "We will stop for refreshments at the edge of yonder wood," said Syntax.

The sun hung high in the brilliant blue Grammarland sky and some of the weaker Words were feeling the heat. The column was becoming extended for a number of Particles (notably, some of the Conjunctions and Prepositions, and at least two Interjections, **Oh**! and **Ah**!) had slowed their pace and now trailed behind the main body of Words.

"We could all do with a rest," observed Josh.

As they approached the wood, a figure emerged from the dappled shade which the luxuriant leaves on the trees afforded to any who stood beneath them.

After his experience with the Giant Oath, Josh felt a quiver of nervousness. Was this to be the next test? His concern was short-lived for, on studying the stranger, it seemed most unlikely that he could be a threat to anyone, least of all to a proud army of many thousands of Words.

"Good day," said the stranger, "and a very fine day it is", he added resonantly. The newcomer was short, plump and rather pompous-looking. He spoke with a fine, cultivated voice, the sound of which gave its owner not inconsiderable pleasure. He wore a crumpled suit which had probably been well-cut and rather expensive when it had left the tailor. But time had taken its toll and it was now decidedly worn and rather out of fashion. The suit was enlivened by an extraordinarily brightly-coloured loosely-knotted tie, marred only by what looked suspiciously like a soup stain. A very fine day, indeed," he intoned, as he attempted without success to straighten his tie.

"Hello," said Josh, for once again it was evident that Syntax expected his young companion to deal with the situation.

"May I enquire what purport you and your most impressionable entourage have in coming this way?" returned the stranger.

"We are on a quest," replied Josh non-committally.

"Could you perhaps be more pacific," returned the pompous one. "Nothing is more quintessential to a Quest, I always say, than the most precise definition of its objective. I meet few strangers in this region of Grammarland - I sometimes feel that people go out of their way to avoid me - and I must confess I am not entirely disinterested in any comings and goings - especially when I conceive the comings and goings, as in this case, to consist of so large a number."

Before answering, Josh looked at Syntax. Unless Josh was mistaken, Syntax's left eye was twitching. It might have been a trick of the sunlight playing on the surface of Syntax's silver face. But Josh thought not. There was a definite twitch.

"I am not entirely sure I understand your meaning," Josh answered the stranger cautiously. "Didn't you mean specific - not pacific? Doesn't pacific mean peaceful?"

"Who knows?" piped up Melisa, whose head was just peering out of the pocket of Josh's tunic. "It may be that he thinks you look rather too warlike and he is asking you to present a less belligerent front. Then again, he tells us he is not entirely 'disinterested' which we must assume means he has something to gain from our arrival. But bear in mind, this truly remarkable fellow is able to conceive with his eyes."

"Good day, Misuse," interrupted Syntax sternly. "I see that you have lost none of your propensity to use the wrong word in the wrong place in the wrong way at every opportunity."

Misuse spluttered indignantly. "That is scarcely the proper way to address one who would be only too happy to help you in your travails. I have always found your hostility towards me entirely beyond my apprehension. Incredulous as it may seem, many, I must tell you, have found my ingenuous use of words exceedingly bemusing."

"I can believe that," muttered Melisa.

"Can you help us?" Josh interjected, since it was clear that Syntax's contempt and Melisa's ridicule were most unlikely to elicit any useful information.

"That," said Melisa, "is rather like a chicken seeking help from a fox."

"It's nothing at all like that!" snapped Syntax whose temper had already been frayed by Misuse and who was in no mood for Melisa's quips. "As usual, your predilection for bizarre imagery obscures rather than clarifies the situation. A fox is a cunning, wily, vicious creature which, when on the loose, has poultry entirely at its mercy. In what way is Misuse foxlike or indeed Josh fairly represented as a chicken?"

"Would that be a poultry objection to my simile?" enquired Melisa innocently. "If not, I will admit you have me foxed."

"Poultry objection!" Syntax growled. "You have clearly been infected by Misuse."

"Could be a case of chicken fox," observed Melisa sweetly.

Misuse took Josh by the elbow and led him to one side. Josh went willingly, realising that the best way to stop the bickering was to remove the mischievous Melisa from the presence of the irritable Syntax. As he walked with Misuse, he casually pushed Melisa back down inside his pocket, an act which prompted a muffled cry of indignation from the garrulous flute.

"If you hope to succeed in your quest," said Misuse, delighted to have a willing listener at last, "I would proscribe a cohesive plan of action. The success of all adventures depend upon precise strategic thinking. First, define the purport of the quest. I have no wish to deprecate your friends but, between you and I, they are more likely to fight each other than any foe who may affront you. How in the event it will all expire, I really do not know."

As Misuse completed his speech, Josh became aware that Syntax was listening to the conversation 'at a distance', using his telepathic powers. 'Far be it from me to interrupt the high counsels of war,' said Syntax inside Josh's head, 'but, to save time, may I be permitted to attempt some modest clarification of Misuse's meaning. I think it is possible that our pompous friend means 'prescribe' rather than 'proscribe', 'purpose' rather than 'purport', 'depreciate' rather than 'deprecate', 'confront' rather than 'affront' and 'transpire' rather than 'expire'. If you effect the substitutions I propose, and you ignore 'between you and I' which should obviously be 'between you and me' and the mismatching of a singular noun with a plural verb in 'Success of all adventures depend', then you will see that the advice Misuse is offering, which had previously seemed incomprehensible and therefore useless, is now revealed as entirely useless in its own right.'

Here, not surprisingly, Syntax paused for breath before concluding; 'You will often find that those who appear to be so rich in Words that they are happy to squander them indiscriminately are, in fact, desperately trying to disguise the poverty of their thoughts.'

Now Josh had to admit that he found Misuse rather difficult to understand. At the same time, it seemed to Josh that Misuse was, at least, well-meaning.

Syntax, abandoning telepathic mode, had by now hopped over to Josh's side. "Well-meaning!" he exploded, "that is the very last thing he is. He is perpetually ill-meaning. He is always using Words inappropriately and incorrectly."

"A pun, I do declare, a pun," squealed a delighted Melisa, who had somehow managed to wriggle her head clear of Josh's pocket once again.

Misuse, stung to the quick by Syntax's insult, was determined to defend his honour. "There are no militating circumstances for your hostility towards me which surely deserves the outright commendation of all right-thinking people. What offence have I perpetuated?" I offer my advice freely. I seek no renumeration. Except perhaps a friendly word."

"My dear Misuse," returned Syntax, "if you showed a little more respect for words, I have no doubt you would find most Words more than friendly. But you trample upon Words; you ask them to perform tasks for which they are entirely unsuited; you cause them the most profound distress. You have just tried to force 'militating' to do the work of 'mitigating' and, in an extraordinary, even for you, example of verbal idiocy, you have substituted 'commendation' for 'condemnation', thus, I assume, saying precisely the opposite of what you mean. As for your offence, you do seem to be perpetuating it in that you persist in committing it, but I think you were really querying whether you had committed an offence at all, in which case you really meant perpetrated. As for 'renumeration' - you leave me almost, but not quite, speechless. There is no such Word, unless you mean the process of renumbering. You meant 'remuneration'. It's from the Latin *munus*, a gift or reward, and nothing at all to do with numbers. Forgive me but I must say it. You have two egregious faults. You are ignorant and you are pretentious. You try to impress those who know no better but you merely elicit ridicule from those who do. If you would only say what you mean in clear and simple terms without cluttering up every sentence with unnecessary Words which would be far better employed elsewhere, you could conceivably become a useful citizen of Grammarland."

"You're being a little hard on Misuse," murmured Josh. "After all, he is only trying to help."

"Your consideration for others does you credit, my boy," conceded Syntax. "And it is true that my nerves are somewhat frayed which shortens my temper. Nevertheless," continued Syntax, slipping into telepathic mode for he did not wish to give further offence to Misuse, nor did he wish to alarm those Words who might be near enough to hear him speak, 'nevertheless, we shall find no help here. Indeed, I shall be frank with you. If we are to succeed, I am afraid that, in the last resort, you will have to find the way without help from any creature living in this land.'

17. Tautology and Family

The army took refreshment and, after resting for an hour, continued on its travels. There was a general feeling of disappointment at Misuse's signal failure to give them precise or even intelligible instructions on where the road was taking them. Indeed **Road** himself became the object of some barbed remarks by the adjective **Rude**, who suggested **Road**'s approach to the Quest was rather pedestrian even for a concrete noun, and some mild verbal abuse by **To Gloat**, who observed that, although **Road** was considered by the army to be an important contributor to the success of the Quest, he currently looked remarkably down-trodden. Syntax confessed to Josh that he now had no idea where they were going, and frowned irritably at Melisa's unhelpful quip that nothing could be more like the great Sentence of life itself.

Josh began to feel depressed. Whereas he had been frightened by the Bog of Disuse, terrified by the Giant Oath (until he had learnt the Giant was so much hot air), and simply baffled by Misuse, he was now overwhelmed by what seemed the sheer pointlessness of the journey and the fear that it might well go on like this forever. As they approached yet another bend in the winding road, **But** (who had been on advance reconnaissance with a party of fellow Conjunctions) came careering back, screeching excitedly "A house! A house!" They quickened their pace and, on turning the bend, saw in the distance a very large tumble-down house surrounded by a circular hedge. "We must see if there is anybody at home", said Syntax. "Perhaps they will be able to show us the way".

When they reached the hedge, they found it was so overgrown that they had difficulty in locating the gate to the garden path. The preposition **Through** was sent to investigate by burrowing his way into the hedge. Eventually the gate was discovered, half buried beneath excess vegetation and sporting a sign, 'The Shambles', held in place by only one nail,. "A name that suits", muttered Syntax, "I doubt very much if anyone has lived here for the last twenty years or more". But as he spoke, they heard a female voice coming from somewhere on the garden path.

"O Cherished One of Mine, phenomena of the audible, and thus, by inference, also of the visual sort suggest that we - not, I hasten to add, that most resplendently impressive of pronouns, the royal 'we' but the 'you' and 'I' conjoined in holy matrimony - have, if you will forgive the abruptness and inadequacy of the expression, visitors."

"Visitors, my sweet Verbiage!" came a male voice in reply, "What an agreeable and thus pleasant surprise. Perhaps we should descend, that is, go down, to meet them."

On hearing this strange manner of conversing, Josh looked quizzically at Syntax, and was about to ask a question, but Syntax put a warning finger to his lips. Down the path came the queerest of couples, a woman of vast proportions who shuffled rather then walked and a tall, gangling man whose limbs, as he moved, described the most tortuous shapes.

"My good friends," the man called out, waving what seemed to be half a dozen hands, "welcome, greetings both cordial and from the heart. It is for me always a delightful pleasure to be here when I have the good fortune to receive visitors. To what, and to whom, do I owe the unrepayable honour of a visit which places me in your everlasting debt?"

Josh was about to reply (guardedly, for once again he was unsure whether the man was friend or foe), but Melisa cut in;

"The honour is entirely ours and redounds to us, in debt forever, eternal, time without end. Pray, may we enquire who you are by asking your name?"

"My name is Tautology," replied the man.

"That's a very peculiar name," Josh whispered to Melisa, "Does it mean anything?"

"Tautology means saying the same thing in different words without adding anything to what is being said, or just plain going round in circles," said Melisa.

"Precisely, exactly, spot on," interrupted Tautology, "or in other words (what would we do without other words!), tautology is tautology. And boys will, I suppose, be boys", he continued turning to Josh. "But say I must when say I must, that pipe you have in your pocket is frightfully clever. I wonder if, using my redoubtable powers of persuasion, I could induce her to help me with my project of circular definitions. But do forgive me, I was forgetting something that had slipped my memory. I'm certain, beyond a doubt, that after your long and protracted journey you must for sure be tired and fatigued. Why don't you come inside for rest and recuperation with a view to reposing and rejuvenating yourselves? I'm certain my better, and, by virtue of her size, substantially larger half would be only too pleased, not to say delighted, to receive you. Not so, my dove?" he said, turning to Verbiage.

"But of course," she replied, "I shall now set off in the mode of perambulatory locomotion along the path, in the direction of the place we inhabit, and, once inside, having attended to those essential bodily functions about which, uniquely, the less said, the better, shall ensure with all due despatch that the devices and arrangements both nutritional and reposeful which you must require shall be placed at your disposal. It is a remarkably agreeable stimulus to my nervous system to be able to enjoy the sensation of being in a position to receive you in our home."

"She means she's glad to see us," Syntax whispered to a bewildered Josh.

"And that she needs to visit the rest room," added Melisa helpfully.

As Verbiage waddled off, Tautology linked arms with Josh (who felt as if his body were being placed in a convoluted noose), and started to follow Verbiage. Syntax ordered **Straight** and

Succinct, another Adjective noted for his brevity, to accompany them (thinking they might come in handy). Neither Adjective seemed entirely happy with this arrangement, but they obeyed. Syntax then instructed the rest of the Words to wait in the garden, while he went with Josh to the house. Both the house and the garden, were huge and appeared to be quite chaotically arranged. The garden which was choked with undergrowth resembled an endless maze and the path that Tautology followed through it was extraordinarily circuitous.

"We don't appear to be going anywhere," Josh whispered to Melisa.

"Nonsense," replied Melisa. "It is obvious our host is leading us up the garden path."

"I am so sorry and do apologise," declared Tautology when, at long last, they emerged from the dense foliage and were confronted by a heavily ivy-clad wall. With a flourish Tautology gestured at what on close inspection was revealed as a door, "Please, if it is agreeable to you, do enter my humble abode, my modest dwelling, where my dear wife and spouse will have prepared suitable refreshments, fitting and most apt for the occasion."

They entered the house and Tautology led them through what seemed an unending series of rooms, until at last they came to an immense dining room. The table was piled high with dirty utensils. Some of the chairs were without backs and some without legs. The walls were grimy and the curtains in tatters. Josh looked around in dismay and wondered if there was a chair both safe and comfortable enough to sit on.

"I hope you don't mind and so won't object to sitting on the floor," said Tautology, "I'm afraid that regrettably everything here is broken. It has been since the Great Altercation between the King and the Queen when they argued with such appalling, not to say cataclysmic, consequences. We somehow never get round to the repair work of fixing things. And because of pecuniary limitations, we are also exceptionally short of money. Still, no point in worrying! Life, in brief, being brief, is short, and thus soon over. Actually, you wouldn't care to sit round me in a circle, would you? You see, I love circles of any sort or kind." Syntax intimated with a nod of the head that he had no objection. "I say, so kind of you, to be so kind," returned Tautology, while making a deep bow, not once but twice.

Adventures in Grammarland

"You have a very large house," said Josh, "I imagine you must have many children."

"Too numerous to mention," replied Tautology, "In fact my beloved spouse has blessed me with such an innumerable number of offspring, or should I say progeny, that I cannot even count them."

"But where are they all?" enquired Josh. "The house seems so empty."

"Oh, wandering about in the garden, I imagine," said Tautology. "You see, that's really my wife's department, save and except when it comes my way. But there she is, with our eldest daughter."

Verbiage appeared carrying an enormous pot of tea. By her side was a neurotic-looking lank-haired creature, bearing a tray loaded with cracked and broken mugs. A bright green parrot was perched on her left shoulder.

"I do entertain the hope that Mr T. is using his very best endeavours to attend energetically and punctiliously to your needs. I must depart your presence now but shall return upon the instant that I have completed my ablutions."

"You mean, you hope he is looking after us?" remarked **Suc-**

cinct somewhat acerbically, despite an obvious, but to Josh inexplicable, nervousness which both **Straight** and **Succinct** had exhibited from the moment they had seen Verbiage.

"And she needs to visit the rest room again," Melisa whispered.

Verbiage ignored **Succinct**'s question and departed with all the speed that her great bulk permitted. On her return, she said; "I bring you potations brewed from the plant with white flowers and oval pointed slightly-toothed evergreen leaves that is grown in China, Japan, India and adjacent countries. And may I now, without further delay, detour or equivocation, come straight to the point" - **Straight** winced at the mention of his name and could scarcely keep upright - "and effect an introduction to the first born of the female side of our offspring, our daughter Digression and her parrot, Whacko. You may call her Di if you so wish – my female issue that is, not the multi-covered avian entity residing on her shoulder. We of course never do 'Di', having a strong aversion to that phenomenon, whose designation I can scarcely enunciate without feelings of acute distress and (do forgive my directness, gentlemen) even nausea - namely abbreviations and short-cuts."

Digression, who had large blue eyes and straggling light-brown hair, giggled and said in a simpering tone, "Oh Mamma I don't think these gentlemen... are you sure you're comfortable on the floor... really does need a clean and the windows... as for the hole in my bedroom ceiling the rain... I do hope the weather tomorrow... I so much wanted... but Papa you don't think we could... such a lovely pony we had ...when I was a little girl you know... in the days when... before it all... remember Whacko?"

"Words! words! words! Shut up! Shut up!" squawked the parrot.

"Pray forgive my interruption," said Syntax who was growing visibly impatient, "but I fear we must soon be on our way. We have far to go and must not delay."

"Oh, that's a bad sign," Melisa whispered to Josh, "when Syntax's words start to rhyme, accidentally of course. I think Digression may be the last straw for the poor old stickler. There is nothing that grates more on Syntax than an unfinished sentence. This girl can scarcely complete a clause, let alone a sentence."

"My dear fellow," said Tautology, "you mustn't mind the

Adventures in Grammarland

ambagious divagations of Digression. They are merely the juvenile high spirits of youthful exuberance. But won't you imbibe the beverage my beloved wife has prepared for you to drink?"

"Indeed," added Verbiage, "If it does not soon make its way down the oesophagus into the lower parts its temperature will decline progressively and inexorably to the point where its capacity to warm the body and cheer the mind will reduce to zero."

"We are grateful for your offer of hospitality," said Syntax politely but with a slight edge to his voice, "I fear, however, we must depart and I wondered whether you might be able to help us on our way."

"The way?" expostulated Tautology, "Good heavens! What a fascinating and interesting topic and one on which I should dearly love to expound by expressing my thoughts upon it. In fact, I have long wanted to grasp and understand the way, but I always seem, nay appear, to get misled into, or should I say waylaid by, path, journey, course, itinerary, route, passage, thoroughfare, lane, avenue, street, trail and track (to mention but a few). 'The way', I fear, is where it is, namely and in fine, nowhere and everywhere. Can't help you there with any assistance, I'm sorry to say. My dear Verbiage, perhaps you have some notions by way of ideas about the way?"

"My superlatively cherished and adored one," replied Verbiage, "am I to understand by your interrogation that on which the foot of man and beast does tread with the purpose of securing a displacement of the body from one site to another, or does your discourse allude to the loftier matter of the Truth, the Light, the Life, the Mystery, in short (to employ an expression I generally abhor but which I shall this once employ, as I see our guests wish to be about their business), the Word?"

Josh asked Syntax if Verbiage's mention of 'the Word' had anything to do with the story Syntax had recounted after crossing the Bog of Disuse. By now Syntax's patience was sorely strained and he replied angrily, "It has as much to do with it as gibberish has to do with useful speech. We are wasting our time here. **Straight**", he added turning to the Adjective who was standing erect with a facial expression composed in equal parts of incomprehension and trepidation, "I am tempted to leave you here to teach these poor benighted creatures a thing or two." **Straight** looked horrified; **Succinct** kept his mouth shut for fear Syntax might decide to instruct him to remain with **Straight**. "But you are indispensable," Syntax concluded. **Straight** heaved a sigh of relief at his narrow escape. Teaching these three to come straight to the point was clearly impossible. And in any case, there was a glint in Verbiage's eye when she looked at him which he found profoundly alarming - not to mention her peculiar habit of licking her lips whenever either **Straight** or **Succinct** caught her eye.

Syntax's outburst reduced Digression to tears - but not, unhappily for Syntax, to silence. She blubbered; "How dare... I mean if you cannot treat my parents... both of whom have been through so much... especially at the time we lost the pony a beautiful animal with long brown ears... you know the kind that are lovely to stroke... when he wandered out into the wilderness never to return... lost in the bog was it... or was it the opposite way in that River with the trolls... or something papa said never go... too dangerous... oh so dangerous... oh is there no end to it... no end to it... no end to it... no end to it? ..."

Digression seemed set on repeating 'no end to it' indefinitely and was joined by Whacko screeching in unison, "Nwentwit, nwentwit, nwentwit..."

Syntax was by now close to breaking point and, from inside his tunic, Josh could hear Melisa subsiding into a fit of uncontrollable giggling.

"Hello," said the tousled head of a boy, peering round the door of the room in which they sat.

"Hello," Josh replied. The newcomer who had now entered the room was about Josh's age and he looked bright and cheerful. "I'm Josh. Who are you?"

"This is my eldest son," Tautology volunteered proudly.

"My name's Drivel," the boy replied. He then addressed his parents. "Sorry I'm late. I've just been down the watchamacallit, trying, like, to sort out the thingamabob with my dubris but when I got there, it wouldn't work and I got a bit sort of, well you know what I mean, so I thought I'd better get back here and see whether I could get a kind of thingamejig, which, like, has got lots of different things on it, you know, which is great, I mean great, if you want to get it sorted."

Verbiage glowed with a mother's pride. "Our guests have been formulating an enquiry which centres upon the identification of an appropriate direction which their peregrinations might adopt. Is it possible that, with your proclivity for embarking on expeditionary adventures, albeit in the area enclosed within the boundaries of the land to which we can claim proprietorial rights, you may be able to proffer advice which will be of assistance to those who have sought hospitality within the confines of the edifice wherein we dwell?" Verbiage enquired of her son, taking advantage of a temporary lull in Digression's babbling.

Drivel seemed embarrassed by so direct a question and, as a consequence, his always limited vocabulary became still further impaired: "Well, I mean, if you ask me, like, I reckon that they ought to get one of those things, you know, which has a thing on it, like, that tells you where the thing that you want to get to is, you know, roughly, sort of thing, as such - but that'll only work if you know what the thing is you want to get to and, like, you know what gizmo you need to get to tell you how to get there, if you get my meaning, if you know what I mean."

Syntax finally lost his temper, "My God, it's like a madhouse here. What this boy says is incomprehensible and can no-one shut that girl up? As for the parrot, I'm sorely tempted to wring its neck."

Tautology and his wife looked most disconcerted by this display of ill humour. Verbiage put one arm around Digression, who was still shouting "no end to it", and the other round the now silent young Drivel. Whacko, still echoing his mistress, fluttered clumsily around Verbiage's head, as though looking for but not finding a satisfactory, resting place. Both the children disappeared into the folds of their mother's copious flesh. Verbiage, accompanied by her engulfed offspring, swept out of the room, muttering; "What may have found its way into the thoughts and feelings of that person completely eludes my consciousness. Were it not that the demands of my corporeal organs must take precedence, I should feel obliged to present my objections in the most forceful manner."

"I know," Josh muttered to Melisa before the flute could speak. "She needs to visit the rest room."

Tautology turned to Syntax, "My dear fellow, pardon me but you must forgive me if I speak with a certain directness, plainly and without circumspection. ("That'll be the day," muttered Syntax, under his breath.) "Not to beat around the bush, I must say without further ado that your own behaviour has left much, indeed and - without wishing to take in vain the name of your worthy colleagues - to be succinct and to come straight to the point, a lot to be desired and, indeed, devoutly to be wished for."

Syntax, who had recovered his composure, apologised for his outburst and, with a tone of impeccable politeness, took his leave. Tautology, who, happily, was easily mollified, responded in equally gracious terms; "Should you ever, at any time, be coming back this way again and be passing "The Shambles", I and my family will be wholly, totally, entirely and unequivocally at your service, without hesitation or reservation."

As Syntax and his party departed, they could hear Tautology bidding them 'adieu', 'farewell', 'au revoir' 'bon voyage' and a string of other words, no longer clearly distinguishable but all of which they were sure meant, in one way or another, 'Goodbye'.

On reflection, Josh felt quite disturbed by their visit to 'The Shambles' for, although he had seen Syntax in irritable, even angry, mood before, he had never seen him lose his self-control.

"He becomes grumpy from time to time," Melisa confided to Josh. "I, of course, have found our meeting here excruciatingly funny. But for Syntax, it has been a nightmare. All those words swilling around with no sense of direction - and so many used where so few would have done."

"One thing puzzles me," Josh addressed Syntax, eager to make light of what had evidently been for Syntax a deeply disturbing experience. "Why did Verbiage...?"

Before he could finish, Syntax replied: "Logorrhoea."

"And what is that?" Josh asked.

"It is an extremely unpleasant and sadly incurable affliction," Syntax replied. "And unhappily Verbiage suffers from it in a particularly acute form. It consists of an inordinate appetite for Words. Hence, the unease of **Straight** and **Succinct**, which I am sure you noticed. The primary symptom, apart from an inability to stop talking, is a frequent need to evacuate her vowels."

"And consonants," chimed in Melisa, happily. "Vowels and consonants."

"Scarcely a matter for levity," Syntax rebuked.

"Sorry," said the incorrigible flute. And then added quickly: "But our time has not been entirely wasted. The girl, in her delirium, said something about a River which lay in the opposite direction to the Bog of Disuse. I think I know what she means."

"Yes," said Syntax, now quite himself. "I too know what she meant. Without of course having the faintest idea what she was doing, I think she may have given us an answer to our question. And it is not good news. If I'm right, we must now face the most difficult challenge of our journey so far."

18. The River of Time

As the shadows of evening stretched themselves across the land, the army reached the River. It was the mightiest river that Josh had ever seen, with a powerful current that churned the surface water into foam as it passed. And it was so wide that only with difficulty could Josh discern the further bank. "Deep it is too," said Syntax, answering Josh's unspoken question. "Deep as thought."

"How on earth are we going to cross it?" asked Josh out loud.

"Well we certainly shan't cross it on earth," quipped Melisa, whose head once more protruded from Josh's pocket. "On a boat, on a bridge, or on the wings of the great eagle that endlessly soars above the Mountain with No Name, perhaps. But on earth, never."

"This," said Syntax, "is the River of Time. We shall rest here tonight so that, in the morning, we are refreshed and as ready as we can be for the crossing."

The army of Words made camp that night on the West bank of the river. They had faced and overcome many dangers and obstacles. Josh thought over their adventures how the ancient **Forswunk** had fallen into Disuse; how the Giant Oath, with his bluster and swearing, had put fear into the entire army, until his emptiness had been exposed; how Misuse, for all his good intentions, had proved entirely useless to those whom he had tried to help; and how Tautology and his eccentric family had revealed the many problems that arise when words lose their way in a maze of confusion. The army had survived it all.

But now they faced a seemingly insurmountable, or rather an uncrossable, obstacle. Josh turned to Syntax. "What is the River of Time?" he asked.

"You ask so many questions," replied Syntax, "and as always I can answer you only in part. The River of Time, as you see, is a mighty river - and a river different from all other rivers in your world or mine - for it flows backwards."

"It flows backwards!" repeated Josh incredulously. "How can that be?"

"No-one has ever reached its beginning or its end. Its source, so legend tells us, is the Ocean of Possibilities. And its mouth lies in a distant Mountain with No Name. The river is a mystery; yet it is essential to the life of Words. You see, we all live in the present, in the 'here and now', so to speak. But the river shows us that there is no here and now; there is only the future and the past. Where we stand, at this point of the river, is for us the present. But the river never ceases to flow. And all the futures we hope for or fear, as soon as they become the present, flow into the past in less than an instant. "The river shows us that there is no such thing as an instant, there is no still point, only the unceasing passage of the future into the past. That is why the river flows backwards, from the vast Ocean of Possibilities of What Could Happen to the narrow mouth of What Has Actually Happened in the Mountain with No Name."

"Well I find all this too difficult to understand," said Josh. "The more I learn of Grammarland, the stranger it seems; a river that flows backwards, with its source in the ocean and its mouth in a mountain; the future flowing into the past before our eyes - and never a 'now'. What does all this mean?"

"That," said Syntax, "is a question which only you can answer. But this much more I can tell you. The river is perhaps the greatest of all barriers. Those who stand on its banks are faced by a terrible threat, the threat of being trapped forever in an inarticulate present where there is not enough time for even a single word to express itself."

"How can anyone be trapped forever in the present, especially if there is no present?" Josh interrupted.

"'To be trapped forever in the present' is what we call a Paradox. It is an expression that seems absurd but which may, nevertheless, be true. I do not blame you for probing the mysteries of Grammarland but I must warn you that the deeper you dig, the more questions you will unearth."

"Well, if the River of Time is so great a barrier, how shall we ever cross it?" Josh asked uncertainly, bemused by Syntax's last answer.

"The situation, though serious, is not hopeless. Let me try to show you." Syntax summoned a nearby Verb to his presence. "This is the Verb **To Be**, an industrious and indispensable Word. Like all the Verbs, he is able to appear in many different forms. For example, he will stand beside the Pronoun I and become **I Am**. In this form, he is the present. But, with no effort, he can represent the future." The Verb **To Be**, unprompted, shimmered for a moment and reformed as **I Shall Be**. "Or again," continued Syntax, "he can represent the past." Once more, **To Be** transformed himself, emerging as **I Was**. "Every Verb can perform such feats. You have already met **To Fight** and **To Conquer**. Well, we **Shall Fight** and we **Shall Conquer** are future forms of those Verbs which, if I may say so, seem particularly apt at this time."

"We **Have Fought** and we **Have Conquered** have an even stronger appeal," chirped up Melisa, who had been listening attentively to Syntax's diligent but not entirely successful efforts to explain the River of Time.

"Let us hope," returned Syntax, taking Melisa's contribution to the conversation seriously on this occasion, "let us hope that one day our young champion will be able to speak those words in all honesty."

"So all the Verbs can work in the future and the past, as well as in the present," said Josh. "That's right", said Melisa. They are simply different Tenses of the Verb. In Clause and Sentence, they can move from present to future and back again to the past."

A number of Words had gathered round, eager to hear their leaders' deliberations. Josh decided to experiment, making use of the willing audience. "If **We Are Brave** in the present," said Josh excitedly, organising a nearby Pronoun, the Verb **To Be**

Adventures in Grammarland

(who was unstintingly co-operative) and an Adjective, "then **We Shall Succeed** in the future and men will say that **We Were Heroes** in the past."

Syntax smiled and then declaimed in a voice loud enough for all the army to hear:

"And a boy shall come from another world into Grammarland, and he shall have the POWER. Then hope shall grow again in the hearts of Words, and Ignorance shall gird his loins for battle against a worthy adversary."

The assembled army greeted Syntax's declamation enthusiastically. "Another quotation from the ancient lore of Grammarland," said Melisa quietly, explaining Syntax's pronouncement to a puzzled Josh. "Dear old Syntax knows every line and every story that make up the legends of Grammarland. Unfortunately, neither he nor any of us fully understands their meaning. But no matter if it encourages the troops."

"But what is this POWER he talks about and why does he think I have it?" Josh persisted.

"After the Great Conflagration, when the wisdom of centuries went up in a puff of smoke, the legend told how Ignorance would rule the land. Thus far, the prophecy has proved true. The Giant Oath, Misuse and Tautology all live in the outlands of what is now Ignorance's domain. Across the River of Time is the heartland of Ignorance. But the prophecy also foretold that one day a stranger, a boy from beyond Grammarland, would somehow enter our world and that, through him and the POWER he possessed, there would be a chance to re-establish order and, well, put things right."

"'Put things right?'" Josh queried.

"Yes, 'put things right'. You see the problem with prophecies is that they are always just a little bit vague. No-one knows what 'putting things right' actually means. But that's the least of our worries. Far more seriously, the prophecy failed to make it clear whether the boy would succeed."

"Oh!" said Josh.

"Not to worry," Melisa continued lightly. "It's not much of a story if you know how things are going to turn out before the end. In any case, first things first, and remember the old Grammarland saying - 'The fastest talker in the world still speaks only one word at a time.' The real question, the one you asked some time ago, is 'how are we to cross the river?'."

"That's right," agreed Josh, "and, like most of my questions, it didn't get an answer."

"That's because Syntax, to whom you addressed the question, doesn't have an answer."

Syntax, who had been lost in memories of long ago, awoke at mention of his name, and joined the conversation. "In the Golden Age," he continued with his explanation of Time, "the river was not an obstacle. Whenever a group of Words formed a Sentence with a Verb in the correct tense, the waters of the River of Time parted, giving safe passage. How this happened was always, in part at least, a mystery. Legend tells us that the greatest gift which THE WORD bestowed on Its creation was the ability of Words, correctly ordered, to master time. With past, present and future tenses, Words enjoyed a unique freedom denied all others. It was only after the Great Conflagration, when the Words became disordered and Verbs confused in their tenses, that crossing the river became difficult."

"Well why don't we put the Words in order," Josh interrupted. "We've done it before, with Melisa's help, - last night, when the argument broke out in the camp. We can do it again. Then, the waters of the River of Time will part and we can cross."

"Perhaps," Syntax replied without any enthusiasm. "But do you realise how long it would take? We have in our company a hundred thousand words and every one must cross. We would have to order every single Word into Sentences. To ensure that every Word made a safe crossing, we should have to bring some of the more versatile Words back from the other side to help those still remaining on the West bank. And every time we brought such Words back, they would need to be accompanied by other Words which had already crossed the river in order to form a Sentence. It could take a very long time, more time than we have."

"Can't we leave some Words behind?" Josh asked hopefully.

"No," Syntax replied emphatically. "The outcome of the Quest will determine the fate of Grammarland forever. We shall need every Word at our disposal if we hope to succeed. In any case, since their very existence may depend on it, every Word has the right to make a stand with us when we face the final test."

"Well that's very encouraging, I must say," said Josh who was after all extremely tired. "We set out on a Quest but we don't really know what the Quest is about; I have a POWER, or so we all hope, but we don't know what it is; and now we have to cross a river and we don't have the first idea how to do it."

"Not so," said Melisa. "Merely because Syntax doesn't have an answer doesn't mean there isn't one."

"Does that mean you know a way?" asked Josh and Syntax in unison.

"Well maybe I do," said Melisa. "In a way, I know a way."

"Come now," said Syntax impatiently. "Do you have a solution or not? This is no time for your foolishness."

"If, when we stand on the very banks of the River of Time, there is no time for my foolishness, pray tell me, dear Syntax, when will there be?"

Syntax emitted a snort of exasperation but remained silent. It was obvious that Melisa was determined to have her moment of glory.

"Well," said Melisa, "there is no way I know to cross the River of Time. The old way is impractical. There is no ford and no bridge. We have no boats and, if we did, the current would sweep us onward into a very uncertain future before we could cross in the present."

"Melisa," interrupted Josh, "We know how we can't cross the river. Can you tell us how we can?"

"Quite right," said Syntax supportively. "If we allow this talkative flute to have her way, we shall be here until the end of time."

"At which time," said Melisa brightly, "it will be quite easy to cross the river since, presumably, it won't be there any more."

"Well, if that's your solution...." Josh trailed off, with a look of disgust.

"Patience," said Melisa. "I don't know a way to cross the river. But I do know a way, a difficult and dangerous way, but a way nonetheless, under it."

"Under it?" queried Josh. "But isn't it very deep."

"Deep as thought," said Syntax, echoing his earlier description.

"Let me explain," continued Melisa, unperturbed. "You have heard from Syntax about the Tenses, future, present and past, that somehow gave Words mastery of the River of Time. But he has told you only half the story. There are other forms that the Verbs can take. There is, for example, the Conditional."

"And what's that?" asked Josh.

"Well, it's not so much about time like the Tenses. It's, how shall I put it, more speculative, more hypothetical."

"Ah yes," Syntax murmured, vainly struggling to recall vague memories of a more ordered world. "It's more a matter of Mood. Less Tense, more Mood."

Melisa could see that Josh was completely lost, so she tried again. "The Conditional is the gateway to a world of infinite possibilities. It is not concerned with what will happen or what has happened at a particular time. When it looks forward, it can explore a limitless number of possible future events, none of which may happen, and when it looks back, it can ponder any number of events which have not but which could have happened. In the future, it is a source of hope; in the past, it is often about regret. Either way, although it exists within Time, the Conditional enables Words to escape the relentless, measured flow of the River. It is the world of what 'could be' and the world of what 'might have been'."

"You mean 'If we could be brave, we might succeed' or 'If only we had been brave, we might have succeeded'"

"That's it," said Melisa, delightedly and with no little relief. "It's all the worlds that have never existed and may never exist, except in the imagination, and the imagination is not constrained by time. That is the why and the how of our crossing of the River. Well done, young friend! Syntax may well be right. There are definite signs of the POWER."

"Oh, no," said Josh. "Don't you start about the POWER."

"No matter," Melisa complied. "Anyway, what I am trying to tell you is simple enough. Beneath the river, there are deep subterranean caves."

"If they are under the river, they would have to be subterranean," snapped Syntax petulantly, frustrated by his failure to recall the precise meaning of Verbal Moods and a little piqued that Melisa, not he, had suggested a way forward. "I fear you may have caught something rather unpleasant from Tautology."

"There speaks Syntax," retorted Melisa, "who has no answers himself and who won't listen to someone who has." Then, aware

Adventures in Grammarland

of Syntax unease at his faltering memory of some the more obscure rules of Grammarland, mischievously she taunted: "Moody and tense. Tense and moody."

"Stop this!" said Josh with a force that surprised himself. "I don't know much, but this I do know. If we three can't work together, we might as well give up now."

The effect on Syntax and Melisa was remarkable. Both looked thoroughly ashamed. In a way, their reaction frightened Josh more than any of the adventures they had so far shared. For the first time he realised that everything really did depend on him.

"Now, Melisa, you were saying..." Josh prompted.

"There are caves beneath the River of Time. These caves, great fissures in the rocks beneath the River, have been opened up by the endless possibilities of the Conditional. Within them, so legend has it, dwell deviants who have found the domination of Ignorance no easier to bear than the old rules of Grammarland. The caves are as dark and damp as the cold and clammy grip of fear and it will take a day as long as the blackest night to cross them. But they do provide a way to reach the other side."

"Very well then," said Syntax, eager to appear positive. He summoned some of his lieutenants, all vigorous Verbs. "Before we sleep this night, every Word, great and small, must be equipped with three torches made of tightly bound brushwood. Now summon **Pitch** and **Tar**."

The summons was issued and, after a few minutes, two swarthy Nouns appeared. "My friends," Syntax addressed the pair, "I have a long night's work for you. By morning, you must treat in your own fashion every brushwood torch so that it will burn steady and burn long when we journey through the caves beneath the River of Time tomorrow. It is a mighty task. Whatever help you need, you shall have."

19. Fortress Dur

On the other side of the River of Times stood Fortress Dur, built on the site of the ruins of the old palace of the Monarchs of Grammarland.

While the army of Words busied itself in preparations for the coming ordeal, in the banqueting hall of Fortress Dur, in the very fastness of his domain, Ignorance, self-proclaimed Ruler of the Land, consumed his third chicken of the evening, bones and all, washed it down with a gallon of mead, gave vent to a belch so thunderous that it made itself heard above the raucous noise of his reveling followers and said; "Then we shall have some sport at last, my friends."

Bigotry, the younger son of Ignorance, responded at once. Since his mouth was full at the time, his remarks were prefaced by a shower of half-chewed meat and vegetables which cascaded back onto the table from which he ate. "They are an affront to Your Majesty and as such should be destroyed without further ado."

Berserk, a warrior whose brutality was a source of unending delight to his commander, rose from the trestle table at which he gorged himself, and, presumably in a gesture of support for

Adventures in Grammarland

Bigotry's proposal, split it in two with a single blow from his huge fist.

Ignorance seemed pleased with Bigotry's opinion and Berserk's spontaneous response. He smiled benignly on his younger son who was using his hands like ladles to recover the lost, saliva-sodden food from the table in order to return it to his mouth. "My son," said Ignorance, "all here know that you are short and fat and have a high-pitched squeaky voice. Less well-known is your undoubted loyalty to me which, second only to your foul-smelling breath, is, in my view, your most endearing quality."

Such insults were considered the highest form of wit in Fortress Dur and Ignorance's remarks were greeted with much laughter and enthusiastic, albeit obsequious, applause.

Prejudice, the older son of Ignorance, tall, thin and of a sallow complexion, scratched his hawk-like nose with a dirty finger-nail. "My brother - short, fat and squeaky though he may be - is right. There can be no room in this land of ours for those who hanker after the old ways. As for my brother's loyalty, my liege, it is, I feel, somewhat less certain and less constant than his malodorous breath."

"Well, well," laughed Ignorance, "Two sons, so different in physique and yet, in almost all things, of one mind. Were it not for their need to compete with each other for my affection, there would be nothing to choose between them. How say you, Havoc?"

Havoc, whom Ignorance favoured above his own sons, gestured graciously with the golden goblet from which he had been drinking. "My Lord's affections must go whither they please," he answered softly, with a knowing smile playing on his handsome features. "As for those now camped on the far bank of the River of Time, of course they must be destroyed. That is self-evident." Havoc paused, running a sensuous hand down the front of the white ermine border of his glistening black cloak, as though he were fondly stroking a dearly-loved pet. "Of more interest, to me at least, is pondering the method of their destruction. I, as you might have guessed, propose a long and lingering death for those who dare to raise their standard against the rule of Ignorance - and therein lies the sport. I have a plan my Lord which will, I hope, satisfy even your most fastidious taste in matters such as this."

"Well I just hope your plans don't involve a lot of planning, that's all I can say," said the pleasantly plump, rather puffy-faced female at Ignorance's side, addressing herself to Havoc. Then turning to Ignorance, she whined; "I see so little of you as it is, O husband mine, and Havoc's schemes always seem to take up so much of your time."

"Fear not, my sweet Stupidity," Ignorance responded in a very kindly voice. "Oh! How I marvel at the wisdom of our Maker who, knowing of your idiocy, gave you such small and piggy eyes and so capacious a mouth!   Small eyes for one who sees and comprehends so little; and an enormous mouth to accommodate both the traffic of boundless nonsense that you emit and the puddings without number you ingest."

This witty sally elicited murmurs of approval from the Court and a self-satisfied grin from Havoc.

"You are too kind," replied Stupidity, who, having failed to grasp the content of her husband's words, based her response entirely upon the gentle and considerate tones in which Ignorance had couched his insults.

"Enough of talk," declared the Ruler of the Land. "'Tis time

Adventures in Grammarland

for the main course. Bring in the lambs. I'm feeling somewhat peckish."

¤¤¤

That night, while the army of Words gathered brushwood, and **Pitch** and **Tar** worked till the sweat ran in sooty streams down their smoke-begrimed faces, Havoc, having refined his strategy of destruction to his own satisfaction, visited the Hangar of Doom to ensure that his mechanics had obeyed his orders. "To the letter," smirked the wiry Grimble, the chief engineer, "indeed, to all the letters". Havoc smiled appreciatively at Grimble's wit. There, in the pallid moonlight, stood a massive engine of shimmering steel. His pride, his joy and certainly his finest creation - the Mighty Shredder. As Ignorance had often said, and Havoc more than any other understood, "A thing of cruelty is a joy forever."

20. The Subterranean Caves

The entrance to the caves lay concealed between two hills that lay back half a mile from the banks of the river. The army wound its way to the entrance in a long column, each Word carrying with him his three torches. Some of the smaller Words, the Prepositions and Conjunctions in particular, had been overloaded when the torches were added to their other baggage, so Syntax had ordered a redistribution of burdens, with the stronger Words carrying some of their weaker brethren's' share. Josh had been pleased to see that Syntax's order had been accepted willingly. Morale was high and there was a growing sense of community within the army.

As the column entered the Caves, the Nouns **Flame** (whose hair was blonde) and **Fire** (whose hair had a redder hue) stood on either side of the entrance, igniting one of the three torches as each Word passed. The descent was steep and the ground uneven. There was much stumbling and the warrior Words suffered many cuts and bruises.

It took more than three hours for the army to enter the Caves, for the lighting of the torches delayed progress. Syntax, as always at the head of the army, hopped this way and that down the dark ravine, seeking out the easiest path for his troops to follow. Josh, marching close behind Syntax, was kept more than busy. Since Syntax had no arms, he could not hold a torch. It therefore fell to Josh to light the leader's path. This in itself was not easy for the energetic Syntax hopped hither and thither and Josh was forced to keep pace with him at all times.

But, still more tiring were the demands that Melisa made on Josh, for the Pipe, with her top protruding from the pocket of Josh's tunic, chattered incessantly.

"Melisa," exploded Josh eventually, having reached the end of his patience. "What is the matter with you? You haven't stopped muttering since we entered the Caves. Half of what you say I cannot hear. And the other half I cannot understand."

"I should perhaps have mentioned," said the Flute in a querulous voice, "that I am slightly claustrophobic. And," she added sheepishly, "I am not entirely comfortable in subdued lighting."

"You're afraid of the dark," Josh accused.

"Everyone is afraid of something," Melisa replied defensively.

Before Josh could explore the flute's phobia further, Syntax signalled a halt. Behind them, thousands of tar-soaked torches flickered in the gloom of the Great Caves, casting vast dancing shadows on nearby rocks. Smoke from the torches curled its way upwards on the long journey to the vaulted roof of the Caves, high above them.

"What is it?" asked Josh.

"There is movement ahead," Syntax replied. "And I am sure that I have seen strange creatures flitting between the rocks on either side of us. We will proceed with caution. Keep a sharp look-out. I think I know who these cave-dwellers are. It is time to light the second of our three torches."

When the fresh torches had been lit and the old ones discarded, the army moved slowly forward. Josh said no more to Melisa, since he was now just as frightened as the pipe. And Melisa herself, having revealed her weakness, fell silent.

"I thought so," said Syntax, as they followed yet another curve in the still downward sloping ravine. "A group of Pedants."

"Pedants?" said Josh.

"They should give us no trouble. They are blind and almost entirely deaf. But we must be careful for, although they mean no harm, they may still endanger our safety."

Syntax hopped on quickly, unwilling to discuss the matter further. But Josh's curiosity was, not surprisingly, aroused by the sad, joyless figures, each of whom hobbled about bestride what seemed to be a broomstick with a horse's head at the top. They looked to Josh like a group of witches, desperately trying but sadly failing to achieve flight.

"They are not quite deaf," said Melisa, helpfully. "Each Pedant can hear what he himself says. It's simply that he can't hear anything else."

"Who are they and what are they talking about so earnestly?" asked Josh, pleased that Melisa was prepared to enlighten him.

"They are a benighted group of individuals who have become obsessed with various aspects of language. Although - prior to the Great Altercation - there was in Grammarland general agreement over the Rules, certain members of the learned professions formed a society to debate the finer points of interpretation. But, as relations between the King and Queen deteriorated, it became a secret society devoted to the cause of making Grammar a totally exact science, governed by logic, from which all exceptions and anomalies were to be expelled. They were not, I might add, taken very seriously, although it was rumoured that the leading members of the society had the ear of the Lord High Chancellor and, even, it was alleged, of the King himself. The hapless creatures you see before you are what remains of that secret society. In the Great Fulmination engendered by the errant Curses, many of the Pedants were to be found milling around the throne of the King and, apart from those who were killed outright, they were, to a man, blinded and virtually deafened by the force of the explosion. Now, they inhabit these Caves where, unbeholden to anyone, they are free to pursue their obsessions. Each, as you see, has his own hobby-horse. As we pass them, you will be able to hear what some of them are saying, if the others don't drown it out."

One of the Pedants, hunched over his hobby-horse and with his head sunk deep into the cowl of his robe, passed them by while intoning;

"Every Adverb should stand by the Verb it qualifies: every Adjective by its Noun. Any deviation from this rule is unacceptable."

A second Pedant 'rode' across the path of Syntax and accidentally bumped into him. The Pedant at once stopped and cried: "Who goes there? You shall not pass until you have answered my question:

"Isn't it about time we ate?"

cannot be correct. It involves the use of a past tense for a future action. It should be 'Isn't it about time we 'eat'?' or 'shall eat?' - or something? Anything but 'ate'. Yes. 'Isn't it about time we shall eat?'. But that just doesn't sound right. So tell me, stranger, what should it be? And speak loudly your reply. I am a little hard of hearing. Oh dear! What did I say? 'Hard of hearing' That's not a very logical expression. I suppose I mean I find it hard to hear but how does that come to be 'hard of hearing'. No one would say 'hard of seeing', though, being blind, I certainly am. No matter, to the point. How should we construe 'Isn't it about time we ate'? Answer me that."

Syntax impatiently brushed the Pedant aside, muttering "There will be a time for riddles when we meet Ion."

"And who is Ion?" asked Josh.

"You will find out soon enough," Syntax replied, "if we ever find our way out of these damnable Caves. Meanwhile, we had best concentrate our minds on present dangers."

The army moved slowly on. Each Pedant they passed repeated the same statement over and over again. Since none could hear what their companions said, there was no agreeing or disagreeing.

"Why do they do this?" asked Josh, genuinely puzzled. "They seem quite intelligent but they are wasting their time."

"Quite right," said Melisa. "That is why they are here beneath the River of Time. Time simply flows over them."

"I see," said Josh, without any conviction. In fact Josh was deeply perplexed by the Pedants' behaviour. He could not possibly accept the assertion of the first Pedant - that all Adverbs should 'stand by' the Verb to which they referred - not if 'stand by' meant literally 'stand next to'. No-one could object to the position of the Adverb Quickly in "The army traversed the Caves quickly". Of course, if 'stand by' simply meant the need for co-operation and solidarity, that was a different matter altogether, but, being self-evident, scarcely merited the energies of a demented Pedant. As for the second Pedant's example of alleged incorrect usage - "Isn't it about time we ate?" - that was more of a problem. It certainly seemed wrong to have what appeared to be a past tense referring to a future action, however clever and flexible the tenses might be. Perhaps it had something to do with what Syntax had said about the Mood of Verbs, but since Syntax had failed to explain this rather obscure matter, Josh could not be sure. In any event, Josh thought the Pedant had asked a perfectly reasonable question and Syntax's reaction seemed rather unfair.

"Idioms, young Josh, Idioms," murmured Melisa, "no point in trying to analyse them. Some of them conform to the rules of Grammar and some don't. That's just how they are. And we would all be much the poorer without them. The Pedants cannot see that this is so and persist with their obsessive and futile analysis. The Pedants are, I am afraid, beyond all possible cure."

Just as Josh hoped that the army would pass by the Pedants

Adventures in Grammarland

without incident, there was a sudden explosion in the middle of the group. A small fissure opened in the rock beneath the one who had been wrestling with the tense of "ate" and a noxious mixture of flame and sulphur erupted into the dark, damp air of the Caves. The Pedant, wooden horse and all, disappeared into the gaping crack. Still declaiming "It's all wrong. It must be 'eat' or 'will eat'", the poor wretch seemed entirely unconcerned at his impending end.

Before Josh could ask Syntax what was happening, another fissure opened, belching fire and smoke. "Move on," Syntax instructed, "Move on quickly. There is no way of knowing how many explosions these Pedants will provoke and, though they harm themselves more than anyone else, as you see it is not safe to stay with them for any length of time."

Neither Josh nor any of the Words needed further encouragement and the entire army scurried past as quickly as possible.

As they left the group of declaiming Pedants behind, now moving ahead on more or less level though still rock-strewn ground, Josh was suddenly confronted by an extremely pallid creature with large, watery eyes and mud-caked hair, who emerged from behind a boulder and stood stock-still, blinded by the light from Josh's flickering torch. The creature spoke.

> "A flider on a gopplegunge
> was gloating on the floy
> when all at twice
> a guth of ice
> beset a saneloi."

"Excuse me," said Josh, taken aback.

"Keep away from him - and warn the Words to give him a wide berth", Syntax ordered. "It is a Babbler. Like the Pedants, he means us no harm but he is nevertheless a threat. He seems innocuous enough but I assure you that his company, over time, could cause substantial damage to your brain. Do not allow any of the Words to approach him. With a mixture of charm and subtle pressure, he will try to lead them off into the darkest recesses of the Caves where they will surely stumble, become lost and almost certainly perish."

"But what is he?" Josh asked, as he obeyed Syntax's instructions, guiding the Words in a detour around the strange, burbling figure.

"Babblers talk nonsense," Syntax replied. "This one is evidently enjoying a rare moment of relative lucidity. Most of the time, they simply emit unintelligible sounds, indistinguishable from grunts and suchlike."

"Why are they here?" asked Josh.

"Unlike the Pedants, who simply perverted the essential task of preserving the Rules of Grammarland, the Babblers have never had a place on the surface of Grammarland," replied Syntax sternly. "Do you remember the story of the origins of Grammarland which I told you after we had crossed the Bog of Disuse, the story of THE WORD?

"How shall I ever forget it?" Josh answered solemnly.

"One version of that great story - for there are many versions - has it that THE WORD emerged from a kind of primordial Murmur. The Murmur covered the world with a sea of undifferentiated sound, from which - so the story goes - the first Word, THE WORD, emerged as a distinct, articulated form. Ah! that moment," sighed Syntax, momentarily lost in mystic reverie, "if only one could have been there to witness it."

"But what has that great event to do with the Babblers?" Josh asked, eager to hear the end of Syntax's tale.

"Well, some say that, as THE WORD emerged, there were other primal entities struggling to move from the sea of sound into articulated speech. They could not succeed. Indeed, in their efforts to emulate THE WORD, they committed the great sin of Hubris. These creatures became our primeval monsters, the demons of our earliest myths. The Babblers, pathetic as they are, are thought to be their descendants or rather a mutant race, harking back to those dark days of our elemental beginnings. So, at any rate, the story would have it. The Babblers play with sound the way children play with mud. They serve as a terrible reminder of what can happen to all those who, while retaining a feeble memory of the Rules of Grammarland, abandon reason in a sea of meaningless sounds, a travesty of genuine words. The final result of such folly is regression to the fearful condition you see here - terminal Babbling."

"Almost as noxious a fate," quipped Melisa, whose spirits seemed to have been strangely revived by the immediacy of danger, "as the Pedantry which afflicts the other denizens of these gloomy Caves".

Syntax gave only a 'Hmphh' by way of reply.

ааа

There is no need to recount all the details of the army's perilous journey through the deepest part of the Caves. Suffice it to say that they encountered several groups of Pedants, all opening fiery cracks in the ground with their obsessions and that, no sooner had they passed the dangers which the Pedants posed, than a Babbler would appear, ever eager to entice the unwary Word into oblivion. Nevertheless, with the aid of the ever-watchful Syntax and Josh who spared no effort to protect them and with the strict obedience which terror imposed, not one Word was lost.

It was now clear that the ground had begun to rise.

"We must be more than half way through by now," said Josh hopefully.

"I sincerely hope so. Our second torches are almost finished and, without light, except for the foul emissions generated by the Pedants, we could wander through these caves, easy victims for the Babblers, indefinitely."

"Oh no!" said Melisa involuntarily. "I don't think I could stand that."

"Why don't we tell half the army to extinguish their third torches now?" Josh suggested. "We can manage with half the number of torches and it will give us a reserve, if we need it."

"An excellent idea," said Syntax and Melisa in unison.

After pausing briefly for a meal, drawn from the packs of rations which every Word had brought with him on the Quest, the army moved forward once more. Progress became even slower, for the ground had begun to rise more steeply but everyone consoled himself with the thought that each step must be bringing him closer to the surface.

"The Pedants and Babblers dwell only in the deepest part of the Caves," said Syntax by way of encouragement. "That danger, at least, is over."

It seemed an age, especially to the claustrophobic Melisa but, after another three hours, Josh saw a pin-point of light, far ahead and high above them. Syntax saw it too. "By the Great Lexicon, keeper of Words, I think we have succeeded."

News that those at the front could see daylight, for such it was, spread back through the column with extraordinary speed and Josh could almost feel the lifting of the army's spirits.

From then, although the ascent was now steep, progress was fast. The Words began to scramble up the incline and Syntax had to enforce a slower pace for fear that some of the Words would injure themselves needlessly or that the weaker Words might fall too far behind. "Bring me the Conjunctions **And** and **But**," he ordered. When the furry creatures arrived, in high spirits despite their exhaustion and full of curiosity to know the reason for their leader's summons, Syntax declared. "These two shall set the pace. Then we shall know that all the army, not just the strongest Words, shall find their way out of this dreadful place."

As they approached the light, Josh noticed with some concern that it was growing dimmer. "Do not be afraid," said Syntax, reading his thoughts once more. "It is now evening in Grammarland. No matter. By the dwindling light of the sun, or by the light of our remaining torches, all of us shall leave these Caves behind us and encamp this night on the further bank of the River of Time."

21. *Evil Observed*

In the banqueting hall of Fortress Dur, Fink, a thin wiry fellow with a sallow, yellow complexion, the most proficient of all Ignorance's spies, added a damp log to the blazing fire. As the fire spat and, to the delight of all, the acrid smoke suffused the air, Fink confided to his master; "The enemy are within the heartland of your domain. They have passed through the Great Caves and are now encamped on the East Bank."

"We could destroy them now," offered Bigotry, hopefully. "They will be tired and unprepared. A sudden attack with all our forces would sweep them back into the River of Time - where their entire army would quickly become a thing of the past."

"Patience, O foul-breathed son of mine," Ignorance replied. "Where is the sport in such a victory, where is their pain that never seems to end, where is their gradual loss of courage as fear tightens its ice-cold grip, where is the turning of their hope into despair? And where, pray, is their surrender to my will and rule? No, no, my impetuous, rotund and most repellent offspring, that is not the way."

ඏඏඏ

In the Hangar of Doom, Havoc, favourite of his master Ignorance, moved with feline fluency around the looming silver shape of the Mighty Shredder. It had surely been in one of nature's less attentive moments that Havoc, so evil, so perverse and so destructive, had been endowed with so much beauty, so much grace. Lovingly, he ran a well-shaped hand across the spiral blade of his latest engine of destruction, following its sensuous curves but skilfully avoiding the razor-sharp cutting edge. He was alone, for Grimble and his team of mechanics had long since finished their final checks. There was, or so it seemed, no-one to see the tears of unadulterated happiness that filled the deep-set, thoughtful eyes in Havoc's handsome face.

ααα

Far away to the north, where the Mountain with No Name rose proudly into the night sky, the wings of the great eagle beat slowly against the thin, cold air as it soared and circled endlessly above the peak. Although so far away and so alone, it saw everything. With sharper eyes than the point of a needle, it saw the army making camp on the east bank of the River of Time; the banqueting hall in Fortress Dur; Havoc fondly caressing his engine of destruction in the Hangar of Doom; - and a boy, who could show courage and fear, who could be cruel and kind and who must use whatever power he had in what would surely be the greatest of all battles, the battle that would seal the fate of Grammarland forever.

22. A Lesson Learned

The camp-fires of the army of Words twinkled like the stars along the bank of the River of Time. Melisa, exhausted as much by her fears as by the journey through the Caves, was fast asleep. Josh knew that he too should rest, for he was tired enough - and who knew what the next day would bring? But he was too excited.

Syntax had spent the evening moving amongst the army of Words, giving advice on how to treat the cuts and bruises so many of them had sustained as they had clambered through the deep, dark recesses of the Subterranean Caves. Now that his work was done, he hopped to Josh's side.

"And how are you?" he asked.

"I think I'm just too tired to sleep," Josh replied.

"You should follow the example of your garrulous companion," said Syntax.

"Did you know that Melisa was afraid of the dark?" Josh asked.

"It was not her fear that I noticed, my boy. It was her courage."

"Well, she didn't seem very brave to me," Josh replied, surprised that Syntax was unwilling to share in his gentle mocking of the sleeping flute.

"Courage, my friend, is not being without fear," Syntax

explained. "It is the conquest of fear. When Melisa told us about the Great Caves, she knew what the journey would mean. She knew that she would have to face her greatest fear, the darkness which is ever eager to devour imagination's light. But she told us nonetheless."

"Yes," said Josh slowly, "I see that."

They both fell silent, for Josh was learning yet another lesson - and Syntax, as ever tuned to Josh's mind, knew it.

After a few minutes, Josh said; "It's funny but I thought you didn't like Melisa very much."

"We are very different, Melisa and I, but we both have a role to play. I am Syntax. I know that without me, there is no sense in Grammarland. I believe in and fight for the rules that made this land great. Without obedience to the rules, the Words become vague, confused and have no chance to reach their full potential. Of course, Melisa makes fun of me. She sees me as a crotchety, old disciplinarian. I know, she calls me 'an old stickler'. But she knows that I am right because, without me, she could never be herself."

"What does that mean?" asked Josh.

"Well, since it is obvious that you are not going to sleep, I will tell you. As you have surely noticed, Melisa loves to play with words. She will make her little jokes. She looks for unexpected and amusing associations between words. When you asked me how I had slept, she answered for me, "Like a log. How else would you expect a stick to sleep?" - do you remember?"

Josh remembered well enough, although he had been sure at the time that Syntax had not heard the flute's quip.

"Well, "like a log" is called a Simile. It means likening something to something else, although the something else is quite unlike the first something in some or indeed many ways. If you want a full explanation, you had better ask Melisa because Similes and their relations, the Metaphors, are not my speciality. I simply mention them because Melisa is happiest playing with words in such ways."

"So, while you are imposing discipline, Melisa is having fun," said Josh.

"You are right, but Melisa knows that without my rules and my discipline, she could have no fun at all. Since she is fast asleep, this much I will admit. She has a way with words which I envy - and the Words love her for it. She has what legend called 'the gift', a kind of magic. In her company, all Words are somehow happier, more at ease. She's fun, that's it. You're right, she's fun. A plodding **Carthorse** passes by and Melisa will, with anagrammatic wizardry, turn it, in the twinkling of an eye, into a fifty-piece **Orchestra** and then as quickly, back again. I've seen her take a Word, like **Deified**, and, with a palindromic spell, make him run in opposite directions simultaneously. She'll make a Pun at every opportunity, often in moments when, to me at least, such flippancy seems grossly out of place. She sees possibilities where I see none. She can create pictures and jokes, where I cannot. All this, I grant. Yet this is also true. Melisa depends on me to give her wit both form and sense."

"In the caves, you weren't very keen to talk about the Pedants. Do they have something to do with the differences between you and Melisa?"

"How observant of you!" Syntax exclaimed. "It is Melisa's view that my zealous protection of the old ways, my determination to see the rules of Grammarland respected and obeyed, may one day lead me into Pedantry. Or rather, it is one of her little jokes. Just as, if I were her, I might gibe her with the opinion that, one day, some of her more florid experiments with Words will reveal her as a nascent Babbler."

"But you're not a Pedant," said Josh. "And Melisa is no Babbler. Between you, you make a lot of sense."

"That is my belief and my hope," returned Syntax.

"In an odd sort of way," Josh added. "I mean odd for someone from the outside world."

Syntax nodded, unsure whether Josh was wholly serious.

"Will we succeed?" asked Josh quickly, before Syntax could use his telepathic powers to probe his mind.

"I don't know," Syntax replied. "But our journey must soon come to an end. Tomorrow, we shall follow this road which will lead us to Fortress Dur, the seat of Ignorance. We will learn nothing from that upstart monarch, but I am certain that we must confront him if we are to succeed in the Quest. Now you must sleep, for tomorrow you will need all your strength."

23. Ion, the Riddleman

There is no sound quite like the noises of an army breaking camp and preparing to march.

The clanking of pots and pans, the chatter and the splashing of the soldiers as they washed the sleep from their eyes in the waters of the river and the shouted orders of the officers drifted back and forth through the cold, grey morning light.

Although this was only his third night in Grammarland, Josh found all these sounds oddly familiar and strangely comforting. "And how are you, my furry friends?" Josh asked of the two Conjunctions, **And** and **But**, who had taken to sleeping, curled up together, at Josh's feet.

"Well enough," replied **But**, "after that dreadful journey through the Caves."

"I thought it would never end," added **And**. "We are only small, so our legs had to work twice as fast as the legs of the bigger Words - just to keep up."

"But, being four-legged, we had twice as many legs," said **But**, "so it balanced out, I suppose."

"And we did have some help," **And** conceded graciously. "Some

Nouns carried our baggage and, once or twice, when we were in real difficulties, the Verb **To Help** came to our assistance."

"But the best part was when Syntax asked us to lead the army. Wasn't that something to remember, eh **And**?" asked **But**.

"And how!" **And** replied.

"But it was still a very frightening experience," **But** concluded.

"Well, it's over now," said Josh. "And today is another day."

"There's nothing like a Platitude first thing in the morning," said a very cheerful Melisa.

"What's a Platitude?" asked Josh.

"It is one of Grammarland's stranger creatures."

Josh thought to himself that it would indeed have to be strange to be considered strange by a talking flute but he said nothing.

"It is renowned," Melisa continued, "for stating the obvious."

"That sounds boring rather than strange," said Josh sharply, suspecting that the flute was making fun of him.

"It is strange in appearance rather than in speech. Rather like a very large duck. Always trying to help with remarks like, 'What's done is done' and 'It never rains but it pours' and 'it's all for the best'."

"I see," said Josh curtly.

"Don't be offended," Melisa soothed, "Platitudes are liked by everyone. The obvious can be a great solace when everything is unpredictable."

"You weren't so chirpy yesterday," said Josh.

"That's true," Melisa replied blithely, "But then, as you said, today is another day."

As soon as the army had completed its preparations, Syntax gave the order to march. Morale was high, for all the Words had concluded, wrongly as we shall see, that, whatever trials lay ahead, none could be worse than the passage through the Great Caves.

"When will we reach Fortress Dur?" Josh enquired of Syntax.

"If all goes well and we meet no more obstacles, we should see the Fortress by noon," Syntax replied.

The road they followed was rough and curved this way and that, but always in a generally easterly direction. The terrain was becoming drier and less fertile. Few plants grew and those that did were of the cacti family. Only vegetation capable of absorbing any available moisture and eking it out through prolonged periods without rain could survive. The ground itself was becoming very stony and the soil between the stones was more sand than earth.

ααα

As they turned a particularly sharp bend, they came across a very ancient figure sitting on a small rock by the roadside.

"Hello," said Josh. "Can we help you?" He was prompted to make this offer of assistance by the deep lines on the old man's face and his long grey beard which suggested that he had lived more years than anyone Josh had ever met, longer even than the ancient Forswunk.

"It is more likely that I can be of help to you," replied the figure in a surprisingly firm voice for one of such antiquity. "I am Ion, the Riddleman."

Syntax signalled to the army to halt while Josh conversed with the old man.

"Why are you called the Riddleman? And why are you sitting on a stone so far from anywhere?" Josh asked.

"I am not sitting far from anywhere," replied the Riddleman. "I am sitting here - and here is the centre of the universe."

"How do you make that out?" asked Josh, taken aback.

The Riddleman laughed. "Every traveller who passes me is

Adventures in Grammarland

allowed to pose one riddle. And you have just posed yours. Here is the centre of the universe because, if the universe is infinite, which wise men say it is, then infinity extends in every direction from where I sit and, if every direction is equally infinite, then I must be at the centre."

Josh was far from convinced by this argument but was more concerned that he seemed to have wasted a golden opportunity. After all, the Quest was a riddle and perhaps the Riddleman could have shed some light on its purpose.

"May I ask one more question?" Josh hazarded.

"No, you may not," Ion answered, sharply. "I am allowed to remain in this Sense-forsaken land on one condition. For each stranger who speaks to me, I may answer one riddle - but one riddle only. If I exceed my quota, the tyrant Ignorance has promised to banish me to the Wastelands, where there is no creature bright enough to ask a question, let alone answer the three riddles which chain me to this rock."

"I don't see any chains," said Josh.

"There are chains far stronger than those made of metal, my young friend. There is hope and fear and despair. Only when my three riddles are answered shall I be free to go my way. So I sit on this rock and I hope someone will solve my riddles, but I fear they will not - and then I despair."

"Well, I don't know if I'm any good at solving riddles and I can't promise anything, but I'm happy to try," said Josh. "So ask away."

Ion looked far from optimistic but he cleared his throat and said;

"What was in the beginning?" is the first of my riddles.

Josh recalled the story that Syntax had told him. Hadn't Syntax said, "Before Time began, which was a very long time ago, there was THE WORD."? Well, in a land of Words, what was more likely to be "In the beginning" than THE WORD"?

"In the beginning was THE WORD."

Josh replied.

A glimmer of hope flashed in the Riddleman's eyes. "You are wise beyond your years. Now I will ask my second riddle. You have given me hope, but hope brings with it fear."

"What broadens as it narrows and narrows as it broadens?" is the second of my riddles.

This one was not so easy. Josh couldn't think of anything.

Unless it was the River of Time. Except that the only odd thing about the River of Time was that it flowed backwards. In all other respects, it had seemed perfectly normal. It just broadened as it broadened and narrowed as it narrowed. Indeed, surely nothing could both broaden and narrow at the same time.

Josh was about to give up when he thought again of that evening when Syntax had tried to explain the mysteries of Grammarland. He had said something about how Words grew stronger in some way when they joined together and how, at the same time, the possibilities became less; how, at the moment when they were most constrained, somehow they were set free. Yes. That was it.

"As a good Sentence grows, the possibilities decrease."
Didn't that sound a bit like something getting bigger and smaller at the same time? And Syntax had also said that, at the very moment the Words of a Sentence are completely trapped, suddenly they fulfil themselves. Well, it didn't really make much sense but it was the best he could do.

"The Sentence broadens as it narrows and narrows as it broadens," Josh gave his answer.

A cry of surprised delight burst from the old man's mouth. "Never, in more years than I care to remember, has any traveller answered two of my three riddles. Is it possible, dare I hope, that this could be the day of my liberation? And yet I fear, for failure now, when I am within a breath of freedom, will bring with it all the terrors of renewed despair."

Josh, despite Ion's fears, was feeling exceedingly pleased with himself. Once again, it seemed, he was proving a match for the challenges of Grammarland. But, inside his head, he heard Syntax warning him not to be over-confident. 'Remember the fate of Pride,' his mentor nagged.

"'Where does the road that you follow end?' is the third of my riddles. Think carefully before you speak," Ion warned, "for more depends upon your answer than you can possibly imagine."

Josh was in no mood to be cautious. Beyond a doubt, he was in good form and the third riddle sounded easier than the first two. Surely, Syntax had told him the night before that their journey would end at Fortress Dur - or, at the least, that the road they were on led there.

"The road that we follow ends at Fortress Dur"

Adventures in Grammarland

No sooner had Josh spoken than Josh knew he had failed. A dark shadow fell across the Riddleman's ancient face.

"I'm sorry," said Josh.

"Hope, fear and then despair," Ion murmured sadly. "Always, at the end, despair."

"Could I try again?" Josh asked.

But Ion was not listening. He had settled back onto his stone to wait for the next traveller who might unravel his riddles and set him free.

"We march on," said Syntax softly. "There is nothing we can do here and we still have some way to go."

The army moved off. Josh addressed himself to Syntax in telepathic mode. "I thought you said that our journey would end at Fortress Dur." There was a hint of accusation in his tone. Josh did not like to fail and he felt Syntax should share the blame.

"I told you at the beginning," Syntax replied quietly, "that all would depend on you. Since you are only too well aware that I cannot answer half your questions, why should you have expected me to be able to solve Ion's riddles?"

"Well you solved the first two," Josh responded rather petulantly.

"So I am blamed for failure but not praised for success," Syntax rebuked him. "But you are wrong. I answered none of the Riddleman's questions. You learned from what I told you and, somehow, you found in what I said the answers to his first two questions. But it was you, not I, who saw the wisdom in my words."

Josh fell silent. Although in the company of a great army, he felt very alone.

"Cheer up," said Melisa, when she knew no one could overhear her, "two out of three isn't bad. I told you that Syntax didn't understand half of what he said. He's a very old stick and his memory, except for the legends and prophecies of the Golden Age, is not what it was. So you can't blame him."

"And you weren't much help either," snapped Josh.

"That's true," replied Melisa, unperturbed. "But it seemed to me that you were relying more on chance than sound advice. I think you were pretty lucky to solve the first two riddles. Correct me if I'm wrong, but you didn't really understand why your first two answers were right, did you?"

Josh laughed. "That's true. I suppose I should be pleased that I had two successes, rather than mope over my single failure."

"Absolutely." Melisa was pleased that Josh's mood was improving. "Only a very great pessimist describes a bottle which is two-thirds full as one third empty. And here's another thought. We all learn more from our mistakes and our failures than we do from our successes. Too often, all we gain from success is pride, but, if we are wise, we can gain humility and understanding from failure - and these are far more valuable commodities."

"But what about the POWER that I'm supposed to have?" Josh asked, not entirely convinced by Melisa's eulogy of failure. "Surely we need to succeed in this Quest? If we fail, we may end up extremely humble and wise but...." and here he faltered.

"But dead," interrupted Syntax as he joined them. "We are approaching Fortress Dur and soon we shall face Ignorance and his band of cut-throats. Now is the time for me to be entirely frank with you."

"What do you mean, 'dead'?" Josh asked with a tremor of fear in his voice.

"This is no game, my friend," said Syntax. "In your world there are battles and wars and men die - and women and children too. Such wars are for land or wealth. No doubt your people think they have their reasons but, to my mind, they are foolish. The land and the wealth it produces cannot be owned. It is merely misappropriated for a while. But here, we are fighting for something far more important. And it will be a fight to the death."

"What is so important?" Josh asked. "I have a right to know. I'm just a boy - and not of your world. Why must I fight in your battle? I'm not a warrior. You have given me a sword, but I don't know how to use it - and it's rusty anyway. This is all a nightmare. Why didn't you make it plain at the beginning that I might be killed? My parents won't like this. And I don't either. I'd like to go home," he concluded with more than a hint of desperation in his voice. And then added, "Now," emphatically - in case he had not made his feelings entirely clear.

Syntax understood Josh's fears and spoke patiently.

"I will tell you what is so important. *You* are so important. That is why I had to bring you here. This is not our battle. It is yours. Melisa is quite right. There are many things I do not understand. But this I know. Unless we win this fight, unless we succeed in the Quest, you and all the children in your world will be accursed."

"Well I'd rather be accursed than dead," said Josh.

"You still don't understand," Syntax continued. "Melisa and I have both told you part of the legend and prophecy of Grammarland. Now I will tell you more, for thus it is written;

> *"One day a stranger, a boy from beyond Grammarland, shall enter our world and shall face the tyrant Ignorance. And they shall fight a great battle. If Ignorance is victorious, his power shall increase a thousandfold and his empire shall extend beyond the bounds of Grammarland into the worlds beyond. Under his rule, men shall speak to each other but none shall understand. And, from the confusion which Ignorance shall foster, death and destruction shall ensue. Prejudice and Bigotry will govern his provinces and Havoc, may his name be feared in this and every other land, shall wreak a terrible revenge on all who stand against him."*

Syntax paused. "So you see, my friend, it is we, Syntax and Melisa and the army of Words, who are helping you in this fight - not you who are helping us. This is your battle, and there's the truth of it. But, know this. We will fight bravely and willingly, to the letter and in the spirit of our lore. We will give our all. This, we swear."

24. The Battle Begins

The road became smoother and broader. "We are entering the Plain of Indifference," said Syntax, "and there," he tilted his wooden body and pointed with his silver head, "there is Fortress Dur."

In the middle distance, across the barren landscape, Josh could see the massive ramparts of an impregnable fortification. "Well, I hope we won't have to scale those walls," said Josh. "We would need ladders as tall as the tallest trees. And, while we were trying, we would be defenceless."

"Well done, my wise young general," said Syntax. "You are right. No-one can scale the walls of Fortress Dur. If it comes to it, the walls must be destroyed, not scaled. But, before we consider how to demolish Fortress Dur, we had best prepare to face its owner - here, on this open plain."

As Syntax spoke, Josh could see the heavy gates of the still distant Fortress open and a column of men, led by a horseman, emerge. "And we shall not have long to wait," added Syntax ominously.

The column grew longer and longer and the drumming of

marching feet and the horse's hooves grew louder, until it seemed the very earth grumbled at the relentless pounding. The army of Words halted and Syntax instructed the troops to form a great square, there, where they stood on the Plain of Indifference. "We shall see what Ignorance has to say but, in the meantime, we must take precautions. If we form a square, we shall be able to defend ourselves on all sides."

"How exactly are the Words to defend themselves?" Josh asked. "They have no weapons."

Syntax replied simply; "The time for questions is over."

The column was now close enough for Josh to see the figure that rode at its head - a large, powerful man, with broad shoulders and brawny arms, his chest covered in an armoured breastplate of bronze, on his head a burnished helmet from which two curved horns sprouted, and at his side, a mighty broadsword.

"That," said Syntax, "is Ignorance."

"I see that our enemy has come better prepared for battle than us," said Josh nervously, making a pictorial comparison of his own rusty sword with Ignorance's weapon and sending it to Syntax telepathically.

"It is the swordsman, not the sword, who wins the battle," Syntax replied.

"And 'A bad workman blames his tools'," said Melisa brightly, peering out of Josh's pocket. "That's a Proverb, a close relation of the Platitude, but rather cleverer. 'It's an ill wind that blows nobody any good' and 'Every cloud has a silver lining'. There's two more Proverbs for good measure."

"Whenever you start to chatter," Josh interrupted, "I know that you are frightened."

"You do me an injustice, my friend," Melisa replied, unperturbed. "The only thing I fear is being trapped in the dark. I am simply trying to help. And, if I am not very much mistaken, it is you who are afraid."

Before Josh could deny the fear he undoubtedly felt, the column of warriors, now well within earshot, halted and Ignorance spoke in a deep, confident and menacing voice.

"I am Ignorance. My empire knows no bounds. I am monarch of Grammarland, Master of all arts and sciences, an orator unmatched in this or any world. I move amongst kings and princes, amongst statesman and priests - and yet, I am equally at home amongst the common people. Now tell me, who speaks for those who have dared to enter my domain without invitation or permission?"

"I am a boy from beyond Grammarland," Josh began. Inside his head, Syntax gave his approval. 'Excellent,' said the silent voice, 'Use what I have told you of our prophecies, for Ignorance knows them too - and fears them.'

"And we have come on a Quest," Josh finished rather lamely.

"What kind of quest might that be?" Ignorance enquired and then waited for an answer.

It was a minute before Josh conceded that he did not know.

"Aha! A quest with no known purpose." There was perhaps just the slightest hint of relief in Ignorance's voice. He laughed and turned to his companions. "A quest! This minuscule, myopic warrior has invaded our territory on a quest. With him, he brings an army of stunted rabble, an army, unless my eyes deceive me, without weapons. What shall we do? Perhaps, before this fearsome threat, we should retreat within the walls of Fortress Dur to cower with our womenfolk. My goodly wife, Stupidity, is ever eager for my company. There, in the ample bosom of her inanities, I could calm my fears, while waiting for my destiny."

Ignorance's sarcasm elicited an appreciative murmur of approval from his troops and no little laughter. After a few moments, Ignorance turned once more towards Josh. Now he spoke in thunderous tones which silenced the merriment of his own troops and sent a tremor of fear through the army of Words. "So you have come on a Quest. Well hear this. There is no point in your expedition - no point at all, for the only discovery you will make at the end of so long and hazardous a pilgrimage is death - a revelation widely available to all with little effort. I will give you one hour to ponder on what I have said. Then, if you do not depart, you shall be destroyed."

With that, Ignorance wheeled his horse round and rode back to a sumptuous tent which some of his lackeys had been speedily erecting during the exchange between their master and Josh.

On reaching the tent, he dismounted.

"Surely you will not let them go?" said Prejudice who, though still unkempt and unwashed, was accoutred in a suit of armour almost as splendid as his father's. "They have insulted your honour and must be punished. Or is the Master of Grammarland becoming soft in the heart or weak in the brain with the passing of the years?"

The blow that struck the side of Prejudice's head was so powerful that it lifted him bodily off the ground. He came to rest some distance away, dazed but still conscious.

"Not at least soft in the fist or weak in the arm?" said Ignorance without any hint of malice. "O my long, lean, and profoundly unclean son, o desiccated fruit, nay brittle branch, of the stout tree of Ignorance, it is only right that you should have your little joke. But so, of course, must I."

Prejudice scowled but said no more.

"I wish the enemy," Ignorance explained, "this host of Words, led by a mere boy, to know what fear is. At the end of one hour, either they will flee or they will stay and fight. Either way, I shall destroy them. But I shall have had one extra hour of exquisite delight to savour their doubts and their foreboding as they attempt to solve an insoluble problem - how to face certain failure and the horror of a brutal death with dignity."

"My Lord has such refined taste in these matters," said Havoc, approvingly. "It is an honour to serve you."

"And serve me you shall," Ignorance responded in affectionate terms to his favourite. "Before this day is done, my sweet harbinger of destruction, you, even you, shall have your fill of serving."

ααα

"We must use this hour to prepare ourselves," said Syntax.

"We might need more than one hour," Josh replied. "How can we fight Ignorance and his troops? His warriors are terrible to behold. Ours, brave though they may be, are of only modest stature. His warriors are armed. They have swords, real swords, and shields. Their leader is mounted and we are on foot. What are we to fight with?"

"Whatever you decide," Syntax replied, "we will obey. You have a hundred thousand Words behind you. And, never doubt, Melisa and I will play our part. But the strategy must be yours. Now, if you have it, you must use the POWER."

"The POWER, again," said Josh. "This power that you can't

describe. And now it's if I have the POWER. I thought you were convinced."

"Before this day is over, we shall know for sure," Syntax replied.

"I always find, when problems are becoming a little onerous, that music can be of help," Melisa suggested.

"A little onerous!" Josh exclaimed. "A host of heavily armed warriors against an ill-organised mass of Words, passing themselves off as an army - this is a problem that has become 'a little onerous'!"

"We are wasting time," Syntax cut in.

"Whatever you think, play," Melisa urged. "Just play."

"Well, it will help to pass the time - and I can't think of anything better to do." Josh took Melisa from his pocket.

No sooner had the flute touched his lips than the most melodious music he had ever heard came forth. The nervousness that had spread through the army of Words subsided and then disappeared.

Nouns and Verbs moved freely amongst each other, giving all they met encouragement and good cheer. Adverbs, Adjectives, Conjunctions and Prepositions all joined in, as a feeling of camaraderie and optimism spread to every corner of the great square formation. "Hail and well met," said **To Fight** to a group of Prepositions consisting of **Down**, **Over**, **With**, **Through** and **Under**. Each Preposition in turn respectfully acknowledged the Verb, affording **To Fight** each time an opportunity to express himself anew. At each obeisance, a Noun or Phrase joined in to give **To Fight** full scope. Even Syntax himself hopped forward when **Under** took his turn, to endorse the new spirit of co-operation which burgeoned amongst the different parts of speech: - "To Fight Down Fear", To Fight Over the Fate of Grammarland", "To Fight With Courage", and "To Fight Through to the End". Then, in a flourish of new-found, if still somewhat ungainly, self-confidence, they joined together in a moving expression of faith; "**To Fight Down** Fear **Over** the Fate of Grammarland **With** Courage **Through** to the End **Under** the Command of the Boy from beyond Grammarland".

From the joyous communion between Nouns and Verbs, new forms sprang forth, part Noun, part Verb. From the Verb **To Give**, **Giving** emerged, at first sight a mere Present Participle, but on closer inspection, a form of the Verb that could stand as a Noun. "It's a Verbal Noun," Syntax explained excitedly inside Josh's head. "'**Giving** alone is enough to give us all hope.' Don't you see? A Verbal form as a Noun with its own Verbal parent, working together. There is fellowship amongst the Words once more, true fellowship."

And, although Josh's mind was absorbed in the fragile beauty of the music he produced, he somehow understood what was happening and knew that it was good.

After a few minutes, Josh stopped. He felt strangely calm. Matters were clear to him now. He must stay and fight. It was, after all, his battle. And he should be grateful for the help, however inadequate it might be, which the army of Words offered.

Josh also felt something else - a new ability to express his thoughts, clearly and simply. It was as though the loyalty of the Words, their eagerness to work together and their willingness to serve him to the best of their ability, had in some strange way energized his mind. Whatever else, he now felt that he could address Ignorance without fear - and that he would never again be lost for Words.

Josh walked amongst the army until he found a place from which most could hear him. "We stay and fight," he said loudly. "We have all seen our enemy. He is strong and well-prepared. But the first step towards victory is to make a stand. And the second is to conquer our fear. These two steps, at least, we can take. When Ignorance returns, I shall tell him that there is not one Word here assembled who will leave the field of battle until Ignorance is no more."

Josh was surprised at his own eloquence. The army of Words was delighted. They cheered until the Plain of Indifference rang out with the sound of their exuberance.

"Well done, my boy," said Syntax. "You have surely given that self-proclaimed monarch something to think about. What are your orders?"

"I have none," Josh replied honestly. "But I would like to spread this message amongst the troops. No-one knows the outcome of this battle. Your prophecy did not foretell who would be the victor or who the vanquished. Therefore, at the least we have a chance. With courage, we shall win."

"There is no need to pass that message," Syntax replied. "The

POWER grows. The army knows your thoughts for they are with you now."

❑❑❑

"I will have your answer," thundered Ignorance, who had returned to the front line of his troops at the appointed time. He had been puzzled and not a little irritated by the sounds of good cheer he had heard emanating from the army of words. "How say you, is it flight or death?"

"It shall be both," said Josh bluntly. "But who will flee and who will die has yet to be determined. Only one thing is sure. We stay."

"The boy speaks with the voice of a man," laughed Ignorance. "What a pity he lacks a man's stature and a man's strength. Were it otherwise, we might have had some sport today."

"We'll give you sport enough," said Josh. "But I should warn you. We did not come to play a game."

"You did not come to play a game," repeated Ignorance angrily. "Oh no! You came on a quest. I see beside you a silver-headed stick. Is that some weapon which you will use in your defence? Or do you have a limp and need the stick's support to help you to make a stand in battle?"

"I am Syntax," Syntax replied in silver tones that carried far across the Plain of Indifference. "I represent the order which you overthrew, the rule which you usurped. This is the day of reckoning and I stand here, beside this boy, to fight for what is right and what you fear."

"I see," said Ignorance. "My trusty sword is to be conquered by a stick in which, it seems, resides a feeble-minded ancient one. I quake."

"And I am Melisa," the flute spoke.

"Good heavens!" said Ignorance in mock amazement. "The boy is a ventriloquist. I could have sworn that voice came from the pipe in this young champion's pocket."

"I am Melisa," the flute persisted. "I too will make a stand this day. It's true I love to play with those old rules which you despise. But I am clever enough to know that, without those rules, my playing would be at an end. We've seen the chaos which your reign has brought. With Stupidity at your side, the crops have withered and all the land east of the River of Time is barren. Nothing that is good can thrive beneath your baleful governance."

"Enough!" cried Ignorance. "I came to fight, not bandy words with talking sticks and waffling pipes. So you believe that there is still a place for Syntax' discipline. And you despise my reign. Well I am perhaps a little smarter than you think. And you are surely fools. From the very beginning, I knew your plans. Each step you took on this your futile journey was reported to me. Did you really think the Giant Oath just happened to confront you; that poor Misuse met you by chance; and that Tautology and all his brood welcomed you to The Shambles out of kindness? Each one was there to challenge, in his or her own way, that pitiable faith you have in the old order. At every turn, my men reported all you did and all you said to Fink, my master spy. I have been with you all the way. And do you still believe the ancient Forswunk simply wandered off the path into the bog? You are pathetic. Behind me now, I have ten thousand more examples of how to break your rules. There's not one warrior of mine who, if he spoke, could fail to make you squirm. But I have had enough of talking. Cold steel speaks louder than a thousand words, as you shall see."

"Do not let him go," said Syntax urgently.

But it was too late. Ignorance's taunt that the feeble, harmless, ancient Forswunk had perhaps been lured to his death by Ignorance had angered and distracted Josh. By the time he had regained his composure, the Usurper had wheeled his horse and was gone.

The battle had begun.

25. The Taking of Melisa

There are some events in any story which it is painful to describe. The army of Words showed great courage and determination, but they were no match for the relentless host of Ignorance which fell upon them with a savage relish for slaughter.

"Neither you or any of your fellows shall see sunrise tomorrow," taunted an enemy commander as he sent his troops through the now broken defensive wall of the army of Words.

"You ain't got no chance," said one of the enemy as he hacked away at an Abstract Noun with his already bloody sword. "We was all looking forward to a good fight but this is child's play."

"If you had learned to run as quick as what them leaders of yours talk, some of you may have survived. Not now, no way!" shouted a particularly vicious attacker, impaling two Words, an Adjective and its related Adverb, with one thrust of his barbed lance.

Josh turned to Syntax in despair. "This is not a battle. It's a massacre. Our troops are defenceless. What shall we do?"

"Play the flute," Syntax replied. "Play the flute and bring some order into our army."

Before Josh could follow Syntax's advice, Berserk, renowned

for his aggression even amongst his fellow warriors in the host of Ignorance, forced his way through the Words who were valiantly but vainly attempting to defend their leaders and swung his mighty fist at Josh, striking him in the chest. As Josh staggered backwards, his assailant snatched at the boy's tunic, cried out in triumph, "I've caught the talking flute" and retreated through the ineffectual opposition of those Words who were still on their feet.

"Oh no!" Syntax exclaimed.

As soon as the news of Melisa's capture reached Ignorance, he galloped to the battle front, now strewn with the bodies of several hundred dead and dying Words, and called off the attack.

"I always say there's nothing like a little exercise to stimulate the appetite before dinner," he quipped, within easy earshot of Josh and the distraught Syntax. "I suggest we take a break. I'm sure our friends will wish to count the cost of meddling in my affairs. We, for our part, will prepare a banquet to celebrate our impending victory."

ㅁㅁㅁ

"He's playing with us," said Josh.

"His playing takes a bloody turn," Syntax replied. "He has captured Melisa and for the first time, I am afraid, truly afraid."

"We're not beaten yet." Josh now felt the full burden of leadership. With Melisa taken and Syntax demoralised, he knew he must find the strength to fight on. He recalled what Syntax had said at the end of their meeting with Misuse: "If we are to succeed I am afraid that, in the last resort, you will have to find the way without help from any creature living in this land."

The Words which had not been injured cared for the wounded. The abstract nouns, as ever more spiritually inclined than their more solid concrete brethren, were particularly active. **Compassion** took charge of the operation, offering the assistance of his fellow abstract noun **Comfort** to all those in need. Meanwhile, Josh concentrated his mind. "There must be a way," he said to himself. We cannot win by fighting. The enemy is better armed and utterly ruthless. But there are weaknesses. Ignorance is vain and reckless. If I can destroy him, we could still win. I'm sure of it. But how?"

◻︎◻︎◻︎

"My Lord, I have a suggestion." Havoc spoke softly in his master's ear.

"Patience, my friend," Ignorance replied. "Your time will come."

"You do me an injustice," said Havoc with a laugh. "I have no wish to shorten the battle or your pleasure. Both, as you well know, could not be dearer to my heart. Rather I wish to heighten the agony and despair of our enemies."

"Then speak."

"This flute, captured by the warrior Berserk, is evidently a friend to the boy who leads the army of Words. It's evident her soft and sweetly sickening voice is a powerful motivator of the boy Josh and the rabble who follow him."

"They will not surrender, whatever you do to me," Melisa interrupted bravely, guessing at Havoc's intent. "The outcome of this battle will determine the fate of Grammarland. Compared to that, what happens to me is of no consequence."

"Bravely spoken!" sneered Ignorance. "My admiration for your courage is tempered only by my contempt for your folly. Might you not be wiser to plead for mercy?"

"It's clear the flute must die," Havoc continued, unperturbed by Melisa's interruption. "But I would like her death to have - how shall I put it - the elegance and subtlety of a fine work of art."

"Go on," said Ignorance, intrigued.

Havoc now whispered in his Lord's ear, so that none but Ignorance could hear. First Ignorance smiled and then he laughed, a wild and raucous laugh that sent a shiver through his own troops, for they knew well its meaning.

◻︎◻︎◻︎

"I bring a message to you from Ignorance, Monarch of Grammarland," said Fink, the master spy, casually waving the white flag of truce which he had brought with him.

"Deliver your message - and then go," Josh replied.

"Against his better nature...," Fink began.

"His what?" Syntax interrupted, contemptuously.

"Against his better nature, the Monarch of Grammarland has

Adventures in Grammarland

decided to release the talking flute called Melisa. She shall go free, free as a bird. On three conditions. First, that you depart this land; secondly that you swear you will never again raise your standard against the rule of Ignorance; and third, most important of all, that you, Syntax, admit that you are wrong and Ignorance, the master of this land, is right. If you fail to agree to these conditions, then the fate of the talking flute called Melisa is your responsibility."

"Tell your Master," Josh replied quietly, "that his terms are unacceptable. Tell him that the flute is a dear friend but that we have come here to fight for the future of Grammarland and all the creatures of this world and mine. We cannot sacrifice their interests, even for Melisa. And tell your Master this. To threaten the life of a defenceless creature who cannot bear arms against the host of Ignorance is the act of a coward. If Ignorance disputes my assessment of his character I invite him to meet me, face to face."

"Is that all?" asked Fink.

"It is." And with that, Josh turned away. And Fink, somewhat disconcerted, departed.

"You spoke well," Syntax comforted. "Melisa is dear to all of us. She and I have had our differences. But we have learned to respect each other. And, if the truth be known, I have grown rather fond of her. Nevertheless, we must stand firm."

"What do you think they will do with her? And why did they make the offer to release her?" Josh asked.

"They made the offer so that we would feel we could have saved her. As to what they will do to her, I cannot guess, but my heart is full of foreboding. My only consolation is that I am sure they would not have released Melisa, whatever we had done. The word of Ignorance is and always has been worthless."

ooo

In the Hangar of Doom, Grimble tended the furnace in which he and his mechanics forged to extremely fine tolerances the metal parts for Havoc's engines of destruction. The furnace was hot, white hot. It was ready.

Ignorance, with Havoc at his side, entered. Behind them strode Berserk, carrying the flute like a trophy, and Fink, still repeating to Ignorance the message which Josh had given him.

"How dare he!" exclaimed Ignorance. "A mere boy. How dare he?"

"Calm yourself," Havoc soothed

"But he has called me a coward, me, Monarch of Grammarland, Master of all arts and sciences, an orator unmatched in this or any world. I move amongst kings and princes, amongst statesman and priests - and yet, I am equally at home...."

Havoc interrupted him, a trifle impatiently. "Yes, my Lord, we know all that." Ignorance's brow furrowed in anger at Havoc's impertinence. But Havoc continued quickly; "It is, of course, outrageous. And he shall pay the price for his temerity. But now, my Lord, be calm. I have a rare pleasure for you - the exquisite pain of an enemy in her death throes immeasurably enhanced by the guilt of her friends who will hold themselves responsible for her agonising demise."

"Very well," said Ignorance grumpily. "But when your little work of art is finished, you know what you must do."

"Of course, my Liege. All, as you see, is prepared."

By now, the party stood as close to the furnace as the heat would allow. "Berserk," Havoc ordered, "give the flute to Grimble."

"But I captured him. Can't I do it?" Berserk protested.

"You lack the skill," said Havoc. "Do as you are told."

"But..." Berserk persisted.

"Berserk," snapped Ignorance, "unless you would like to share the fate of the flute to which you seem so deeply attached, I advise you to obey". And then he added to Havoc, "Discipline is slipping. We shall have to do something about it when this battle is over."

Berserk reluctantly handed the flute to Grimble.

"You may destroy my body," cried Melisa bravely. "But my soul is the music which I produce. My music is but a breath of air on the wind - and that you cannot destroy."

"Are we going to spend all day listening to our own men arguing with us and our victim giving her own funeral oration," said Ignorance impatiently. "For Chaos' sake, get on with it."

Grimble placed the flute in the jaws of an extremely long pair of tongs and asked those assembled to stand back. Smoothly, he swung the tongs in a wide arc towards the furnace. "Now we shall hear some music," quipped Ignorance. "Sing your last song. And I hope your screams carry to the furthest corner of your pathetic little army of Words."

The base of the flute was now at the very mouth of the furnace and already the silver base was red hot.

"She begins to melt," said Havoc complacently.

"But she's not screaming," Ignorance complained.

And it was true. As Grimble very slowly slid the flute, base first, into the furnace, there was no scream.

But there was a sound - a sound that floated up through the chimney of the furnace and out from the Hangar of Doom, a sound that did indeed carry to the furthest corners of the army of Words, a sound of music, so sweet, so subtle and so soothing that it touched the hearts of all Melisa's friends and made even her enemies in the host of Ignorance fall silent and listen in amazement. Only Ignorance and those who stood beside him in the Hangar of Doom, all entirely absorbed in their evil machinations, failed to hear that gentle melody, enriched by a thousand thrilling harmonies. Deaf they were to the song of Melisa in her passing, a song that surely augured ill for the demonic schemes of her tormentors.

A trickle of molten silver, all that was left of poor Melisa, crept from the small spout at the base of the furnace. "Gather the metal carefully," Havoc commanded the wiry Grimble. "And forge me an emblem, in the shape of a skull. Affix it to the front of the Mighty Shredder in such a position that all those in its path shall see the death's head, fabricated from the body of their late lamented friend, the moment before the blades do their work."

"When you've quite finished," said a still ill-humoured Ignorance, "I look forward to seeing your latest device in action." Josh's taunt of cowardice still rankled and the destruction of Melisa, which had failed to engender even the briefest of screams, had done little to assuage his anger. "And I just hope," he added ominously, "that it will fulfill, if not exceed, all my expectations."

"Do not worry," replied Havoc smoothly, "When have I ever disappointed you?"

26. Melisa's Passing

The music that emerged from the chimney of the furnace in the Hangar of Doom and drifted across the field of battle had a most extraordinary effect upon the army of Words. Both Josh and Syntax knew that it signified the end of their friend but, at the same time, they realised that Melisa had, somehow, triumphed in her moment of death. It was clear to them that the spirit of Melisa, the 'gift' as ancient Lore described it, had been released and was now free to float in the wind, to make music wherever it went, from the ghostly remains of the Northern Castle in the east to the land far to the west, whence the expedition had set out, from the Ocean of Possibilities in the south to the Mountain with No Name in the north. Although her body had been destroyed, Melisa would now be with them at all times and in all places, a friend to help and comfort them, beyond the reach of her enemies, and theirs, forever.

27. The Mighty Shredder

The Mighty Shredder was almost as tall as the Hangar of Doom itself, a bright, shiny engine of ultimate destruction. Grimble lovingly polished the newly minted death's head (now fixed in position), slid carefully down the sloping side of the machine and leapt nimbly to the ground beside the eager Havoc.

"You have done well," said Havoc, "You shall be well-rewarded. To you I give the honour of driving my latest and my greatest device into battle." He said no more, for his heart was full and only with great difficulty did he manage to suppress tears of pride and joy. "This is my finest work," he said eventually, almost choking with emotion. "Be sure that you are worthy of it, Grimble."

"Well, shall we see what it can do?" Ignorance said sharply. "Destroy them all. But leave the boy and his talking, walking stick for me."

Grimble, deeply moved by the honour which Havoc had done him - sorry only that Havoc had not announced the honour before he had dismounted - began the long, difficult and dangerous climb up the gently sloping sides of the massive steel body. "We should have attached a ladder to the side," he mumbled.

"What, and ruin the aerodynamics and aesthetics, at one and the same time!" Havoc exclaimed, outraged.

Eventually, Grimble reached the driver's cabin safely and settled himself comfortably in the seat. Havoc signalled to him to proceed. The gates of the Hangar of Doom swung open, revealing the battlefield in the distance. Grimble touched the starter pad in the instrument panel. There was a whirring noise and the Mighty Shredder purred into life.

▫▫▫

They saw it as soon as it emerged from the Hangar, a great silver shape, moving slowly and relentlessly forward. "Good Heavens," Syntax exclaimed. "What is that?"

"I don't know," Josh replied. "But I certainly don't like the look of it."

As it drew closer, they could see the whirling spiral blade set low in the front of the machine, like the teeth in the gaping mouth of an enormous, ravening shark. Anything in its path was caught by the blades and minced.

Some of Ignorance's troops, keen to inspect the latest invention of their master's favourite, approached too closely. A powerful suction from a slot beneath the engine's mouth, almost at ground level, caught them and pulled them towards the whirring blades. Grimble made no effort to stop or even slow the machine and the wretched warriors had their curiosity satisfied in an exceedingly gruesome fashion.

"Are you well-pleased, my Lord?" Havoc asked of the self-styled Monarch of Grammarland, as they followed in the wake of the Engine of Destruction.

"It works well enough," Ignorance conceded. "'Though I would prefer you to direct its energies against our enemies. Eager as I am to encourage unquestioning obedience amongst our troops, slicing them into small pieces seems, even to me, somewhat excessive."

"Fear not," Havoc laughed. "Grimble is simply running a field test. He knows what he must do. He will not stop until all our enemies are defeated, on this battlefield and to the furthest borders of your Kingdom. And, should you so wish it, far beyond."

Adventures in Grammarland

By now, the Mighty Shredder had reached the battle-front and terror spread amongst the army of Words.

"If we are quick on our feet," Josh shouted to his demoralised troops, "we can dodge it or outrun it."

But he was wrong. Grimble turned the power up to '2' on the control panel and the force of the suction doubled. Grimble smiled as some of the slower Words felt themselves caught. Chuckling gleefully, he ran his hand lovingly over the control panel, confirming that the suction scale ran from '1' to '10'. He would leave it at '2' for now. But, if he chose, on suction level '10', he could catch objects a mile or more away. The whole army of Words was within his grasp, however fast they ran.

The first victim of the Mighty Shredder in the army of Words was the Adjective, **Handsome**. Grimble had set the blade to 'rough cut' and Handsome was simply sliced in half. To Grimble's surprise, his victim, although strangely altered, was not killed. Out of the machine's vent on the left side shot a Noun, **Hand**, while on the right, a highly versatile, if non-descript, Word, **Some**, fell to the ground. Both words picked themselves up and hurried away from the infernal machine, apparently little the worse for their abrupt transformation, although **Some**, somewhat dazed, seemed unsure whether to present himself as an Indefinite Pronoun, an Adjective, an Adverb or even as a Noun.

Ignorance, who was watching the Shredder's performance closely, turned to Havoc and expressed his dissatisfaction. "If the only effect of your horrendously expensive machine is simply to double the number of my enemies, you and I shall have to engage in a little chat when this battle is over."

"Teething troubles, mere teething troubles," Havoc replied, still unperturbed.

Grimble adjusted the blade on the Shredder to give a finer cut. The next victim was the Abstract Noun, **Despair**, who, having decided there was no point in trying to avoid the inevitable and who was in any case mesmerised by the silver death's head affixed to the front of the Engine of Death, simply waited for the Shredder to take him. On this occasion, there was an even more remarkable transformation, for, from one of the vents, an entirely new word emerged, **Praised**, the past participle of its parent Verb **To Praise**. **Praised** preened himself a little on his successful passage through the Shredder and wandered off towards a crowd of admiring Words.

"My Lord," said Havoc quickly, "obviously we have not been able to conduct a full test of the machine inside the Hangar of Doom. Be patient and, as soon as Grimble has mastered the controls, you shall have your heart's desire."

Grimble turned the dial to 'fine cut', moved the suction control to '4' and began his work in earnest. Hundreds of Words were now sucked into the Shredder and many were entirely dismembered. But it was far from a complete success. With so many Words going through the machine at any one time, some escaped with relatively minor injuries, others still managed to reform themselves into new Words. A rather scruffy Adjective **Untied** was transformed into a much better organised and effective Adjective **United**. The Adjective **Ill-fed** who, with a life-time of poor diet behind him, had found the rigours of the Quest especially harsh, actually benefited from his passage through the Shredder, emerging replete and content as the Past Participle **Filled**. Of particular note was the Abstract Noun **Violence**, who somehow emerged in two parts, from the left vent as a rather vague but pleasant Adjective **Nice** and from the right as another Abstract Noun, **Love**. Ignorance who, on the advice of Fink, had already identified **Violence** as a likely convert to his own ranks was not, it need hardly be said, amused.

"Enough, enough!" Ignorance finally exploded with anger. "You are making me look a fool. For every one Word you destroy, you are transforming another into two. I would rather rely on my trusty sword. Recall Grimble and we shall launch a full attack. There is no substitute for the cut and thrust of hand to hand fighting."

Havoc felt frustrated but he dared not challenge the undisputed Master of Grammarland. A messenger was sent to recall Grimble.

In the meantime, Ignorance ordered his host of warriors to prepare for the resumption of the slaughter by more conventional methods.

"Perhaps before the final annihilation of your foes," said Havoc, "my Lord would like to make an example of the boy who has offended you. His humiliation in front of both armies would make a fitting prelude to your ultimate triumph."

What motives prompted Havoc's suggestion, we can only guess. No doubt the prospect of seeing the audacious child broken in full view of the army of Words appealed to him. At the same time, Havoc perhaps thought that the boy might put up a good fight. If he did, then Ignorance himself might suffer some mild embarrassment when his own host saw that its leader had to struggle to subdue a mere boy. There could, after all, be no glory in such a victory. That too might give Havoc some pleasure since he was piqued by Ignorance's criticism. No one, least of all the Master of All Arts and Sciences, should pour scorn on Havoc's most ingenious, grandest and most expensive invention.

Whatever Havoc's motives, Ignorance responded favourably. "An excellent proposal. Just what I had in mind." Ignorance laughed in that tone which inspired fear amongst all who knew him.

ooo

Far away in the Mountain with No Name, the rhythmic beating

of the wings of the great eagle stopped for a moment and the bird, in silent mastery of its high domain, soared without effort on the rising currents of air. Suddenly, the silence of the Mountain was broken by a terrible shriek. It was the eagle's battle cry.

28. The Final Confrontation

"Where is the boy that dared to call me coward," Ignorance bellowed.

"I am here," Josh replied. Syntax spoke to Josh inside his head. 'This is the time,' Syntax told him. 'Now we shall see who has the POWER. Remember all I have told you and, more important, all you have learned. Remember Melisa, and the insight she gave you into the true potential of the Words. Remember that we are with you.'

"Draw your sword, bespectacled boy," Ignorance demanded. "Draw that piffling little blade which, unless my eyes deceive me, is the only weapon your impudent army possesses, and prepare to die."

Clearly, Ignorance intended to mock Josh before killing him. Ignorance's own sword, now unsheathed, glinted threateningly in the afternoon sun. It was a massive broadsword, honed to a razor-sharp cutting edge on both sides of the blade. Josh's sword, on the other hand, was, as Josh well knew, short, blunt and rusty. Nevertheless, Josh drew it, for to refuse might be interpreted as surrender.

As the short blade slid from its sheath, Josh heard a sound that thrilled and delighted him, a sound that drifted back and forth across both armies. It was the music of Melisa. "I too am with you," said the flute's melodious voice. With Syntax at your side and me in your heart and head, the POWER shall be yours. It is my gift to you. Look more closely at the weapon in your hand. Use it wisely and use it well. For victory can be yours."

Josh was so happy to hear Melisa's voice again that, at first, he failed to notice the strange transformation of the blade he held. First, it became suffused with a brilliant white light; then it shimmered in all the colours of the rainbow; finally, in a swirl of a thousand delicate hues, it dissolved in Josh's hands, sending a gentle, strangely warming glow through his whole body. Suddenly Josh penetrated another of the mysteries of Grammarland. For the Sword he had despised was not an inferior weapon. Deftly touched by the spirit of Melisa, it had become W O R D S. "Yes," said the singing of Melisa, "so light a touch, so great a change. The only limit to your POWER now is your ability to use it." At last Josh understood that the weapon Syntax had given him, the only weapon he would need, was Words. Words, in a land of Words, must be the most powerful of all forces. He did not lead an army of defenceless creatures. He lead the most glorious army known to man. The army of language.

And he also knew that, just as Melisa had shown him how to deal with the Giant Oath, so now the spirit of the flute had hinted how Ignorance himself might be overcome.

"I am told by Fink that you doubt my courage," Ignorance taunted.

"Would you not agree," Josh replied, "that anyone who revels in the destruction of those whom he believes to be weaker is cowardly?"

"I am Ignorance...," the Monarch of Grammarland began.

"You are a usurper," Josh interrupted and then added forcefully. "I can see into you. I know you."

"And what do you see, urchin?" Ignorance roared. "For, if you see clearly, you see your death."

The strength of the POWER grew within Josh and he began to explore the true nature of his enemy, probing him, taking him apart, playing with him, remaking him.

"I see **A n g e r**. I see **I r e**. I see **R a g e**. That much is obvious."

"They are but words, boy?"

Adventures in Grammarland

"In a land of Words," Josh chided his adversary, "the Monarch should show more respect for his subjects. But that is not the point."

"What is the point, pray?" Ignorance asked.

"**A n g e r**, **I r e** and **R a g e** are all words that come from the darker side of human nature. And they are all to be found within you."

Ignorance was taken aback. The army of Words behind Josh gasped in admiration and delight. Even the host of Ignorance began to murmur as the truth began to dawn.

But Ignorance was not beaten, far from it. "Simply because you faced three of my lackeys - the Giant Oath, Misuse and Tautology, all abusers of the values you hold dear - you must not think that you can conquer Ignorance. I concede that you have learned much. But there are deeper mysteries than those you have uncovered. Until you find the answer to Ion's third riddle, I am invulnerable."

The murmurs amongst the host of Ignorance subsided. They knew that their master was right and that, if, as seemed almost certain, he was victorious, there would be a high price to pay by those who had doubted, even momentarily, his invincibility.

Josh too realised that he must not be over-confident. He returned to his dissection of Ignorance. "I also see within you a sign that you can be defeated."

"What sign is that?" asked Ignorance cautiously, for it was now evident that he had a worthy adversary.

"I see **G r o a n**, the sound of complaint, of pain, of despair. Lurking within you is the knowledge of the wrong you do and a fear of retribution."

"What else do you see, boy?" Ignorance barked, hoping that soon the child's ingenuity would be exhausted.

Josh laughed. "I see some hope for you."

"You dare to mock me!" Ignorance exclaimed.

"Oh yes! I dare," Josh replied. "You still do not understand. I have the POWER, not you. Look closely." Josh probed once more, concentrating with all his might, for this time he explored his enemy fully. Inside his head, he could hear the blood pulsing through his ears, beating rhythmically, like the wings of a great bird. With ease, he rearranged the whole essence of Ignorance in the pattern of an eagle's outstretched wings. "There," he cried in triumph. "With the POWER, I can turn you inside out. I can compel you, who feel for no one but yourself, to deny your very nature.

```
I  G  N  O  R  A  N  C  E
C  A  R  I  N  G  O  N  E
```

Behold, the **C a r i n g   O n e**".

There was total silence for a minute while all those assembled studied Josh's latest attack. Syntax spoke first. "It is true. He has taken Ignorance in the palm of his hand and re-fashioned him more to our liking." Then the army of Words cheered, for they too saw that it was so.

"Well done!" said Melisa in Josh's ear. "I'm proud of you."

"And I owe so much to you," Josh called out to the blue sky above.

Ignorance could see that victory was slipping away from him. The old prophecies were all jumbled inside his head. "A boy, a worthy opponent, the POWER!." But no, it could not be so. Before he had even met this wretched child, the boy had failed. He had not been able to solve Ion's third riddle. Therefore, he could not succeed. That was why Ignorance had chained the Riddleman to a rock at the edge of the heartland. Ignorance was no fool. He knew he could be beaten. So he had placed Ion there, to interrogate all newcomers. If any had succeeded in solving all three riddles, Ignorance would at least have been forewarned. But all had failed, all, including this boy. "Not so fast, my little sprat," Ignorance said in a quietly menacing voice.

"Where does the road you follow end?"
"Answer me that, and answer now. If you fail, our little talk, the quest and your life - are at an end."

"Think carefully," Syntax urged. "None of us can help you now. This is the final test, the final mystery. This is the purpose of the Quest."

"Remember all that has happened since you joined us on the Quest, and may you find the truth," said Melisa's voice.

Josh shut his eyes and once again concentrated with all his might. He recalled his first meeting with Syntax. "Where am I?

Am I awake or dreaming?" he had asked. Syntax had replied by asking him exactly what he meant. He thought of the army's confrontation with the Giant Oath, Misuse and Tautology - all, in their different ways, had shown the same essential flaw. Syntax and Melisa had taught him much on the journey - how, if words were correctly ordered, they became more powerful, how there were rules which gave strength, how those who understood the rules could be set free and enjoy all the pleasures of the imagination.

Ignorance interrupted his chain of thought, demanding with growing confidence an answer to his question.

"Where does the road you follow end?"

But Josh would not be hurried for he knew that everything depended on his answer. He ran through in his mind's eye his meeting with Ion. He studied the first two questions which the Riddleman had asked him. He recalled his correct answers - THE WORD and the Sentence. Then he remembered, from Syntax's story of the Golden Age, the King's demand that the Queen keep to the point and the Jester's remark "Let us hope the point will prick, quickening sense into good sense." And Syntax had said: "There's is little point in going on a Quest unless we are able to defend ourselves". And that reminded him of Melisa's remark after the Giant Oath had exploded - about how the point of the pin could destroy the biggest balloon. "It's the point of the pin that's the point of the pin," she had said. And Ignorance himself had said something about a point - "There is no point in your expedition. No point at all." - and he had said it with a hint of relief in his voice. Somewhere in all this lay the answer.

And then he knew.

For the third time, and, surely, by his tone the last, Ignorance roared;

"Where does the road you follow end?"

Josh answered in a voice that rang out as clear as a bell on a still summer's day.

"The road I follow ends in a POINT."

"Why did you give that answer?" Ignorance asked in a shaking voice.

"Because if you look to the end of a long straight road, it ends in a point. Because after the Words of a Sentence, there is a point - a full stop. Because the Words in a Sentence must make a point. Because the POINT of the Quest is MEANING," Josh shouted triumphantly. "And because MEANING is the POINT of the Quest."

There was a moment's silence. Then Ignorance let out a dreadful howl of rage and despair.

ααα

In the Mountain with No Name, the eagle which sees all and understands all, beat the air with its powerful wings, climbing higher and higher. When even the mountain peak was far below, and the whole of Grammarland was spread out beneath it like a patchwork quilt, the eagle shrieked three times. It was the cry of victory.

ααα

Not far from the eastern bank of the River of Time, Ion, the Riddleman, sat alone and half asleep, chained to his stone by hope, fear and despair. Suddenly, he looked up. What was that eerie, distant sound? Had he imagined it? No, there it was again. By now he was wide awake. He stood up. For the third time, he heard the eagle's cry. The chains were broken. He was free.

ααα

Precisely what happened on the field of battle remains confused to this day. Havoc, realising that all was lost, ran to the Shredder which Grimble had abandoned near the Hangar of Doom and clambered with great agility into the driver's seat. Turning the engine on and setting both the cutting blade and the suction to maximum power, he set out on his last great orgy of indiscriminate destruction. He made short work of the entire Host of Ignorance, sweeping backwards and forwards through the ranks. Yes, the Shredder worked. Grimble had simply been too cautious.

Ahead of him, Havoc saw the figure of Ignorance, defiantly waving his broadsword at the Shredder as it approached. With a curl of satisfaction playing on his lips, Havoc pressed the acceler-

Adventures in Grammarland

ator and Ignorance was caught by the powerful suction. With a sudden whoosh, the Usurper's feet shot from under him and he hurtled feet first into the spinning blades.

Ignorance himself was quickly consumed but his sword, which entered the machine last, proved less digestible. The blade of the sword, like the blades of the Shredder, had been tempered from the hardest metal that Havoc and his engineers had been able to forge. When the two equally hard metals met each other, the Shredder seized up. Unhappily for Havoc, who had not envisaged any such possibility, there was no cutout device and the inward workings of the machine, deprived of fodder from outside, began to feed upon itself, consuming its own body, metal panels, shafts, chains and all the other materials of which Grimble had so carefully constructed it.. The driver's cabin, with the driver still in it, was the last morsel it savoured, before what was left of Havoc's greatest invention exploded.

And, struck by the shock waves of that explosion, the impregnable walls of Fortress Dur began to crumble, trapping and then crushing all within it.

Josh, who was watching this extraordinary process in amazement, turned to ask Syntax why the suction power of the Shredder had failed to affect any member of the army of Words. But before he could speak, just at the moment when the remains of the Shredder exploded, there was a flash of light beside him and there, in the place of the familiar silver-headed stick, stood a tall, silver-haired, straight-backed gentleman.

"Who are you?" Josh blurted out.

"I am the Lord High Chancellor of Grammarland. And I am your old friend, Syntax."

"But, but..." Josh repeated incredulously.

"Patience my young friend, and I shall explain all," the venerable one continued. "You remember the story of the Golden Age which I told before we set out on the Quest. Well, when the magic of the spells that the King and Queen aimed at each other collided, I and Selima, the King's daughter and, most unusually, the court jester, stood in their paths. The King had intended to turn the Queen into a small silver figurine. The Queen had aimed to turn her husband into a wooden stick. On impact, the magic became all muddled up. Selima became a silver flute with a wooden mouthpiece - yes, Melisa. And I was trapped in a wooden walking stick with a silver head. All very undignified!"

"But how did you free yourself?" Josh asked.

"Well, if I can take any credit at all, it was because I chose you to lead us. The moment Ignorance was discredited, the spell began to weaken. All his power, over me and the whole army of Words, was at an end. That was why Havoc could not harm us with the Shredder. Even the Words that Grimble destroyed while the Usurper ruled are now free to reform unharmed. When Ignorance was finally destroyed, with all his rabble, I was at last set free."

"We've won, haven't we?" Josh said happily. "You, Melisa and me."

"Or should it be 'You, Melisa and I?" Syntax replied with a laugh.

29. The Victors Rejoice

I need hardly tell you that there was great rejoicing that night. The Words knew that once again the rules of Grammarland held sway and that all now had the chance to express themselves in a world of real, not illusory, freedom.

In innocent delight, Sentence after Sentence formed - clear, precise, unambiguous. Nouns and Verbs greeted each other, with unalloyed relief, like old friends from whom a fearful curse has finally been lifted. And, after so long a time, the poetry and prose of the Golden Age flooded back into the collective mind of the great assembly, rhythm and rhyme, metaphor and simile, yes and pun too, all now free to disport themselves, in robust or subtle mode, within the generous confines of well-ordered thought. Words knew once more the delight of complete fulfilment in Meaning's willing service.

And Syntax, or should I say, the Lord High Chancellor, told a tale or two of the Golden Age, giving, as we might expect, due emphasis to the need for clarity in thought and speech, a need best satisfied by deference to the values which he represented.

And, above it all, with sounds so delicate and fine, Melisa sang a song which promised all the revelers the unparalleled ecstasy of exploring the imagination, flying on the wings of inspiration as high as they liked, as high, if they had strength and courage enough, as the great eagle that circled forever the Mountain with No Name.

ooo

It was not until long past midnight that Josh had the chance to raise with Syntax a matter that troubled him.

"My work here is done," said Josh. "I have made many friends, especially you and Melisa, and I shall never forget you. But now is the time for me to return to my own world. I miss my parents and I have so much to tell them."

"I foresee one or two problems, my boy," said the Lord High Chancellor ponderously. "First, if you are able to return to your own world, you must tell no one of your adventures here, for no one, or almost no one, will believe you. Secondly, it may be a little difficult for you to find your way back."

"What!" said Josh. "I mean why?"

"Well," replied Syntax in a serious tone, "when you left the Library, I told you to bring something with you that was yours in your world and which would help you to return."

"Yes, I remember," Josh said slowly, as the problem became clear to him.

"You took the flute," Syntax continued. "Unfortunately, Melisa cannot help you. Her spirit lives, but her body is no more."

"What about you? You came with me from the Library," Josh asked, close to panic. 'There must be a way back,' he thought. 'There must be.'

"But I didn't belong to you. In any case, I could help you only if I resumed the form I had when we set out. Even if I could do it - and I have no magic powerful enough - you would not wish me to be entrapped once more in the undignified guise of a walking stick. Not when I have just regained my freedom after so many, many years."

"Well I can't stay here," Josh cried. He was now more afraid that at any time since he had entered Grammarland.

"There is a way," the Lord High Chancellor paused, with just the hint of a smile on his usually stern countenance, and even, for a moment, the slightest suspicion of a twinkle in his eye.

"How? Tell me how."

"You brought with you the most cherished possession of any being from your world. It was the thing we needed to succeed. It was the reason I summoned you."

"What is it?" Josh asked impatiently.

"It was your mind, your human mind. You had within you the seeds of understanding. You acknowledged, even if you did not fully know, the importance of Meaning. That was the POWER."

"Well, if that's all, why didn't you tell me in the first place," said Josh grumpily. "I was really worried."

"I did not tell you at once because this is the most important lesson of all," the Lord High Chancellor replied. "And I wished you to understand it. It is the mind that opens all doors - in this world and in yours or, for that matter, between the two. Remember this lesson well. Men may try to accumulate possessions, to amass wealth, to dominate others. But the only possession of any worth, the only real wealth and the only true power is the power of the mind."

Syntax surveyed Josh's thoughts. The boy still did not fully understand but he would learn.

"Go now," said the Lord High Chancellor of Grammarland. "You will fight many battles in your life. Some you will win and some you will lose. For that is the way in both our worlds. But remember this. You have confronted the greatest of all enemies, Ignorance, and have conquered. And also remember this. Both Melisa and I shall be with you all the days of your life. Melisa's spirit is now free to ride upon the wind. Where the eagle flies, there are no boundaries, neither between countries, nor between worlds. As for me, I must stay here, for there is much to do, but happily you and I can always converse, mind to mind, if not face to face. The glasses you have worn throughout the Quest, the glasses that enabled you to see my world as I see it and not as your kind see me and mine in yours (if you follow me), are all that hold you here. Give me the glasses and, as I promised so long ago, you will find yourself back in your bed before you woke. Go now and may the POWER of Words be with you."

Josh removed the spectacles and handed them to Syntax. And then he blinked.

30. The End

Josh awoke in his bed. He felt thirsty. He could hear the faint murmur of his parents talking downstairs. He crept out of bed and opened the door a few centimetres.

"Is all well?" Mr Ware asked the departing Mrs. Brown.

"Everything's fine," Josh heard Mrs Brown's reply. "Josh went to bed at nine. And he hasn't stirred since."

"Good night, Mrs Brown, and thank you," Mrs Ware said. "Wrap up. There's a summer gale blowing out there."

"Well that was an evening well spent," said Mr Ware to his wife. He was standing in the hallway and Josh could hear him clearly.

"He's doing well all round," Mrs Ware mused, "but it is worrying that he is not very interested in English Language."

"Especially when his mother is such an eminent writer," Mr. Ware laughed, and then added, "He can't be good at everything. In any case, they didn't say his English was poor. Just that he wasn't very interested. You know, when I was his age, I felt very much the same."

"Really!" said Mrs Ware, genuinely surprised. "You've always been such a stickler for the correct use of English. What converted you?"

"That's a long story," Mr Ware replied, with a strange look in his eye. "But I can tell you this, it was quite an adventure." And then he added with a laugh, "So I'm a bit of a stickler, am I? Well, may be that's not really so very surprising."

"I still think it's worrying, Arthur," Mrs Ware persisted. "If he's not interested, he won't learn. It's no good being brilliant at all those other subjects if he can't express himself. Anyway, I think we should talk to him about it. At least explain why it matters."

"Talk to him by all means," Mr Ware agreed. "But I think you will find any day now that what you have to say is - how shall I put it? - music to his ears."

"Are you taking any of this seriously?" Mrs Wise asked, perplexed by her husband's apparent lack of concern.

Josh stood at the top of the stairs.

"You're supposed to be in bed," his father said.

"I felt thirsty," Josh replied.

"All right," his mother intervened. "Come downstairs for a few minutes. I'll get you a drink. And I want to have a word with you anyway."

While his mother and father busied themselves in the kitchen, Josh slipped into the Library. To his intense disappointment, the old silver-capped walking stick stood in its accustomed place. With a sinking heart, Josh opened his flute case. There, sure enough, was the flute. "Could it really have been just a dream?" Josh asked himself. "It had been so vivid."

"Josh," his mother called. "You are naughty. You can't be thirsty. You've drunk almost a full bottle of orange squash."

ooo

When Josh returned to bed, he felt extraordinarily tired. Why his mother had decided to lecture him on the importance of English language in the middle of the night, was far from clear. If his father had not rescued him, he would still have been downstairs. "Josh has taken the point unless I'm very much mistaken," his father had said. "Off to bed now." As Josh had left, he was almost sure his father had winked at him. That in itself was odd, for Mr Ware was certainly not a man much given to winking.

◻◻◻

Just before he drifted off into a deep sleep, Josh heard, or thought he heard, through the window-pane the gentlest, sweetest and most melodious of sounds riding on the wind.

◻◻◻

Whether the Quest had been a real adventure and not just a dream must, I suppose, remain a matter of conjecture. To those who demand concrete evidence before they believe in anything, we must admit there is none. The walking stick and the flute were still in the Library, apparently unmoved. As for the matter of the orange squash - who can tell? Evidently, Josh had not imagined going to the kitchen for a drink. But that proves nothing, for perhaps, his thirst quenched, he had returned straight to bed. And that was when the dreaming had begun.

◻◻◻

Even the two marks on the bridge of Josh's nose had almost faded by morning.

THE END

The Parts of Speech

(All Words appearing as characters in the story are printed in heavy type in upper and lower case.)

THE NOUNS

Abstract Nouns
Anger
Despair
Doubt
Forethought
Hope
Ire
Love
Point
Rage
Truth
Violence

Concrete Nouns
Fall
Fire
Flame
Flint
Groan
Hand
Hedge
Hero (as plural Heroes)
House
Pitch
Road
Sea
Sky
Something
Sun
Tar
Tent
Wood

THE PRONOUNS

He
Me
Mine
Thee
Thou
We
You
Yours

THE ADJECTIVES

Bald
Blind
Brave
Bravest (superlative)

Exhausted
Forswunk (Obs)
Handsome
Hurt
Ill-fed
Nice
Pilgarlic (Obs)
Quick
Rude
Some
Straight
Succinct
Untied

THE VERBS

To Be
To Challenge
To Fight
To Forgive
To Fribble
To Gloat
To Mock
To Persist
To Praise
To Search
To Share
To Stammer
To Succeed

PARTICIPLES

Caring
Filled
Praised
United

THE ADVERBS

Gruffly

Quickly
Truly

THE PREPOSITIONS

Down
Over
Through
Under
Up
With

THE CONJUNCTIONS

And
But
If
When

www.ingramcontent.com/pod-product-compliance
Lightning Source LLC
Chambersburg PA
CBHW030444300426
44112CB00009B/1149